HOW AMERICANS VIEW MORMONISM

Seven Steps to Improve Our Image

Gary C. Lawrence

Foreword by Senator Robert F. Bennett

Published by
The Parameter Foundation
PO Box 12076
Orange, CA 92859-8076
435.477.8400
www.parameterfoundation.org
www.howamericansviewmormonism.com

ISBN-10: 0-9820391-1-5
ISBN-13: 978-0-9820391-1-3

Printed in the United States of America

To Jan

Table of Contents

Foreword

One of my favorite authors, when I was a young man, was a humorist/cartoonist named James Thurber. He wrote a number of books, which he illustrated himself. The one that comes to mind as I contemplate Gary Lawrence's work on current perceptions of Mormons by their neighbors was entitled *Fables for Our Time*, in which he did his best to bring Aesop up to date. It told the following story, as best as I can recall:

A weaver and a silkworm met each other on the road. The silkworm showed the weaver some of his silk. As he handled it, the weaver asked, "Where do you get this stuff?" The silkworm replied, "You wanna make something of it?"

They parted in anger, each sure he had asked a perfectly logical question only to be insulted in return.

I don't recall Thurber's moral to that story, but the exchange has stuck with me all these years as an example of how often people miscommunicate – both as speakers or listeners – without ever knowing that they are doing it.

For politicians, such miscommunication can be fatal. To help us avoid it, we hire experts like Gary Lawrence to help us understand what our listeners are really thinking, so that we won't say something we think is reasonable only to discover that what our hearers took away from our comments was something very different than what we thought we said.

No one uses the methods of research to dig into these problems better than Gary. I have used his work in both business and politics, and know that he knows how to get to the meat of what people really think. I am delighted that he has now chosen to put his tools to work to try to help Mormons understand how other Americans really view them and their Church.

Elder Neal Maxwell once said to me, "The prophets always prophesied that the Church will emerge out of obscurity and darkness. As that is coming to pass, some members of the Church are finding that they prefer the obscurity." Maybe so, but we cannot stop what is happening; we can only seek to understand it and respond to it with wisdom. The research that Gary has done will help us do that.

Senator Robert F. Bennett
Washington, D.C.
Summer 2008

Acknowledgements

Thanks first and foremost to my wife, Jan, for her encouragement, love, and support, as well as to my children Stephanie, Kristen, Matthew, and Lindsey, and my sons-in-law Ben Smith and Ben Miller. Their interest in and excitement about the book kept me going.

To a good friend and benefactor who played a pivotal role in the production of this book, but did not want to be mentioned. There, I didn't mention you.

To my editor, Christina Reeve, for patiently questioning phrasing and structure. Any violations of the rules of written English will undoubtedly be where I did not follow her advice.

To Bob Bennett for his generous comments in the Foreword.

To reviewers who graciously gave a boost to this first-time author with the blurbs found on the back cover.

To Terry Jeffers for his cutting-edge ideas about information technology.

To my media gurus – Grant Baird, Kieth Merrill, Ron Stone, and Mitch Davis – for their insightful discussions with me about new ways to use mass media ... and when to jettison the old.

To my stake presidency – Matthew Goodman, Hal Williams, and James Graham – for keeping me focused on what best helps the members.

To Mike Lowe, who tightened my writing in a kind way.

To my fellow LDS pollsters Ron Hinckley and Vince Breglio for their help in analyzing the survey results.

To Dan Williams for his statistical analysis.

To Ben Rancie at Jet Creative for the creative cover design and book layout and Damien Bear for assistance with photography.

To Charlene Beecroft, Colleen Bedford, and Mary Kay Peirce for proofing the manuscript.

To my colleagues at Western Wats telephone center for their professional interviewing and data processing. Lisa Adair, Robert Maccabee, and Marilyn Bajao were especially skilled team leaders.

To the many who took the time to read the manuscript and offer suggestions, among them: Paul Ashton, Greg Christofferson, Shellie Frey, Glen Greener, Jay Haldeman, Bruce Hughes, Ralph and Shauna Johnson, Jenny Johnson, Jack Rushton, and Ron Wilson.

Introduction

>
> People have a right to their own opinions, but they do not have a right to their own facts.
>
> - Senator Daniel Patrick Moynihan

We Mormons – members of The Church of Jesus Christ of Latter-day Saints – have a major image problem.

- Few Americans have an accurate understanding of who we are and what we believe.
- The resulting ignorance is causing increasing antagonism and fear of us.

It is a premise of this book that we have taken too lightly the seriousness of our poor public image. We know that truth will eventually prevail, and many of us, therefore, have become lackadaisical in doing anything to help it. As a result, the misconceptions, distortions, and untruths being told about us have slowed the growth of the Church, and many lives that could be blessed with the truths of the Restoration are not being blessed.

I believe we can turn this situation around if we change the ways we relate to those of other faiths.

When I left on my mission to South Germany, I was a math major; when I returned, I found myself in the social sciences. My mission experiences opened a fascination with how people think and why they behave as they do. As a result, my undergraduate studies in political science, my graduate education in communication psychology, and my professional life for 35 years as a pollster have focused on the study of attitudes and behaviors – how they're formed, how they're measured, and how they're changed. Through hundreds of focus groups and surveys, I have studied why people vote as they do, why they watch what they watch, why they believe what they believe, why they buy this brand over that, and many other issues in which attitudes and behavior intersect. And year after year, the thought always on my mind was, "How can what I'm learning about human behavior benefit the Church?"

The answer is this book.

It explains in plain terms that **friendly and natural conversations, the facts, simple claims, individual latitude, non-threatening invitations, and gentle mentoring** are the ways we can combat distortions, improve our image, and spread the gospel.

I hope you will find it helpful.

Although I have conducted many focus groups and surveys for the Church over the years, the opinions in this book are my own. I do not present them as, or imply that they are, the views of The Church of Jesus Christ of Latter-day Saints.

Gary C. Lawrence
Santa Ana, California
Summer 2008

Words, Questions, Answers

When I had heard these words
I began to feel a desire for the
welfare of my brethren...

- Enos

Words move people. And the right words in the right settings, confirmed by the Holy Ghost, change people.

"There was a war in heaven," my dad said as he taught me about our pre-earthly existence and the purpose of life. It had only been a few years since he had returned from service as a Marine in World War II, so it was natural that his 10-year-old son immediately imagined a great battle with planes, tanks, and bazookas. What a war it must have been, I thought.

How deflated I was when he corrected me and told me the implements of that special conflict were . . . words.

Words? That's it? Just words? How exciting could that have been? I liked my version better.

But I soon began to grasp the importance of this hinge event in our existence and the "weapons" we used to defend the principle of agency and God's plan for the happiness of His children. And I grew to understand that this war has not ended, that only the battlefield has changed.

So as the battle continues, we may wonder how to fight this war. We know the task this time will be even tougher because . . .

- we no longer dwell in an environment of truth and knowledge;
- we no longer use a pure and undefiled language;
- we no longer have a memory of our past; and
- we no longer live in the immediate presence of God the Father and His Son, Jesus Christ.

A difficult setting, to be sure, but the work is doable and necessary. To help us with this challenge, this book will answer questions such as these. . . .

7

Why don't people understand us?

How much do people really know about us?

What is our image as Mormons, and why?

What Mormon vocabulary might be difficult for others to understand?

If we have an opportunity to say only one thing, what should it be?

When referencing other faiths, should we talk about similarities or differences?

How can we talk about the Church without feeling uncomfortable?

On what doctrines do people agree with us more than they agree with their own clergy?

How bold should we be?

Who should control the learning process?

How can we better use technology?

What should be our reaction to negative buzz about us?

When should we continue talking and when should we stop?

How should we correct misperceptions and distortions?

What can members do that our mass media messages cannot?

What is the easiest way to tell others what we believe?

What is the major impediment to interest in the Church?

How can we improve our image from our homes?

How does improving our image differ from missionary work?

How many Americans can see themselves seriously investigating the Church at some time in their lives?

Is there a role for pressure in our efforts?

The Situation

Overview

 Research is simply to find out what you are going to do when you can't keep on doing what you are doing now.

- Charles Kettering

In February 2008, Lawrence Research interviewed 1000 randomly selected Americans by telephone and asked them an average of 24 minutes of questions about Mormons and Mormonism,[1] a substantial research project by any measure. Many of the questions I included came from years of wondering how people really view us deep down and, to the best of my knowledge, have never before been posed to a cross-section of Americans. Results of the more than 160 variables my firm measured will be found throughout the book, but the next four chapters present the main findings – **the gratifying, the sad, and the infuriating**.

After analyzing these survey results, plus findings from other polls and focus groups, I submit there are six general groupings of feelings and perceptions that shape the problematic side of Mormonism's image and standing in America.

The Ignorance Factor. Questions about our basic beliefs – whether we are Christians, whether we believe the Bible, our relationship to Jesus Christ, acceptance of historical Christian traditions, the role of Joseph Smith and other prophets, etc. – are driven mostly by a simple lack of knowledge, although some ill will may be involved.

The Polygamy Factor. The key word is confusion – confusion about the facts, confusion about history, confusion about breakaway groups. It has become an excuse not to entertain further information.

The Power Factor. The central suspicion and fear about us is whether we would use force to reach religious goals. This is fed and exacerbated by the negative traits a sizeable segment of Americans believe apply to us.

The Weird Factor. We are a people apart and we are different, as the Lord intended, and the unfamiliar – from our belief in a pre-mortal existence to our ordinances for the dead – might be seen as weird, as the things of God are often foolishness unto the world. These are generally harmless impressions, but if people also harbor suspicions about power, then weirdness will feed it.

The Secretive Factor. Centered on rumors about temple worship, this factor becomes a problem the more we keep to ourselves. Even positive traits such as self-reliance and taking care of our own can contribute to this perception if we are not involved in our communities.

The Exclusionary Factor. Any time a prophet delivers to the world the message God has delivered to him, it follows that the prophet will be mocked and that those who believe him will be viewed as thinking themselves better than others. Antagonism often follows.

Let's examine the research and uncover the underlying concerns Americans have about us.

Exposure to Mormonism

 New opinions are always suspected, and usually opposed, without any other reason but because they are not already common.

- John Locke

As I prepared to leave on my mission, my father, who served his in Australia, said I was fortunate to go out at a time when missionaries no longer had to hold street meetings. He told me how he dreaded them and how he cringed as he and his companion stood atop orange crates on a busy street corner and, obedient to instructions, sang a hymn, followed by a prayer and a sermon, hecklers notwithstanding. He said he felt like a nut, and was sure the people who passed by would not have disabused him of his self-perception.

At least, as the reasoning went, the pedestrians were exposed to Mormonism. Yes, but the Church eventually saw that this method – a vestige of London's Hyde Park tradition – did not reflect well on us, and was discontinued.

There is exposure . . . and then, there is exposure.

Friends and Acquaintances

All but 2% of the nation have heard of Mormons, but when asked how many individual Mormons they personally know, the non-LDS portion of the sample told us . . .

Number of Mormons Known

do not know any
37%

know one or two
21%

know several
32%

know a lot
10%

Groups

Highest groups* with many Mormon friends:

Residents in the West, post-grads, divorced, 18-24-year olds, above $50K income, never attend church services, non-Christians

Highest groups without Mormon friends:

Less than high school, minorities, Baptists, Northeast, Evangelicals, widowed, Midwest, 35-44-year olds, under $50K income

*The highest groups are those that significantly exceed the average result for that answer category and may not necessarily constitute a majority of that demographic or religious group.

Combining these findings with answers respondents gave us regarding the activity status of their Mormon friends, here are the exposure statistics:

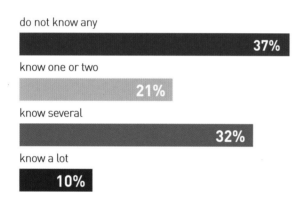

Activity of Mormon Acquaintances

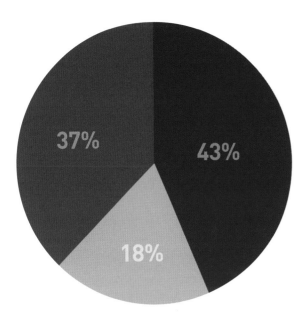

■ **43%** know at least one active or devout Mormon

■ **18%** know one or more Mormons, but none that are active

■ **37%** do not know any Mormons

In other words, **55% of all Americans do not know an active member** of the Church. A majority of Americans have never knowingly rubbed shoulders with a practicing Mormon, which will go a long way in explaining why we're having problems. What we should do about it is quite obvious:

"They need to be less hidden and more public."
(Man, Washington State)

"They need to publicize their religion a little more, and say plainly what they stand for, so that we know who and what they are."
(Man, Arizona)

"They should not be so quiet. Be more out there so people can understand."
(Woman, Kentucky)

"Get people to know Mormons as people and not as a religion."
(Woman, Washington State)

Groups

Highest groups knowing an active Mormon:

West, some college or more, above $50K income, no religious affiliation, very liberal, 25-34

Highest groups knowing only an inactive Mormon:

Catholics, non-Christians, 25-34, somewhat liberal, high school graduates, Northeast, below $50K income, senior citizens

Media, Missionaries, and Literature

In terms of other sources of exposure to Mormonism . . .

Exposure to Mormonism

Have seen Mormon ads on TV

71%

Have been approached by Mormon missionaries either at their homes or someplace else

62%

Have been given literature from Mormons

59%

Combining these three items, we find that **84% of our fellow Americans have had at least some exposure to Mormonism** through our ads, our missionaries, or our literature, or all three.

Groups

Highest exposure to TV ads, missionaries, and literature:

Upper-educated,* West, Republicans, 35-54, above $50K income, both the very liberal and the very conservative, married

*College graduates and post-graduates as a group.

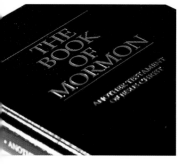

Conversations and the Internet

We are only in the beginning stages of using technology to inform others who we are and what we believe. The survey found that ...

Conversations and the Internet

27% of those outside of our faith claim to have had a substantial religious conversation with a Mormon other than the missionaries.

27%

13% have Googled or otherwise looked up something about Mormonism on the Internet.

13%

3% have received an email from a Mormon friend with information about Mormonism. As expected, these recipients are younger and better educated.

3%

Groups

Highest groups looking up Mormonism on the Internet:

18-34, college and post-grads, liberals, West, singles

Lowest groups looking up Mormonism on the Internet:

Seniors, widows, low education, 35-44, Catholics, Baptists

Those highest in claiming to have had a substantial religious conversation with any Mormon, not counting the missionaries, are residents in western states, post- grads and college grads, 25-34 year olds, liberals (both very and somewhat liberal), and those making more than $50,000 per year.

Those who are least likely to have had substantial conversations with a Mormon are the opposite: less-well-educated (high school or less), residents outside of the West, seniors, widowed, singles, and making less than $50,000 per year.

The farther away from Utah a Mormon lives, the greater the need to reach out to neighbors and become known.

In short, we have good exposure from our TV ads and our missionaries, mixed exposure to our members, some participation in serious religious discussions with a member, and little exposure so far through the Internet and email.

Images of Mormonism

 A city set upon a hill cannot be hidden from the world, but that doesn't mean it cannot be misperceived.

After the 1964 U.S. presidential election, Senator Barry Goldwater, the Republican nominee who lost to President Lyndon Johnson, complained about the stories that had circulated about him during the campaign. He is reported to have said that if he hadn't known this Goldwater guy better, he wouldn't have voted for him either.

We Mormons know how he felt as we hear stories about us that are, to put it charitably, a little short of the truth. Though we would prefer a rosier environment to work in, we must understand how Americans view us so we can figure out how to correct misperceptions and mistaken identities.

Name Impressions

Sometimes we members think that although the world may not be beating a path to our door, people generally respect us. Unfortunately, that is not the case. **Our image is upside down**. It was bad enough at the beginning of 2007 when Gallup reported that 42% of Americans held a favorable impression of us and 46% an unfavorable one,[2] but events during that year have driven our numbers down even more: only 37% of those outside of our faith now view us favorably, and almost half (49%) have an unfavorable impression of us, as shown in the table on page 24. What is even more disconcerting is that **for every person who strongly likes us, there are more than four who strongly dislike us.**

Of six religious groups tested in our February 2008 survey, we are next to last. In other surveys I have conducted in various locations in the nation, only the Muslims and the Jehovah's Witnesses have a worse image than we do.

The image held of Jews is an interesting comparison. They, like us, are only 2% of the population and have not always enjoyed a positive image, but they now have a solid, almost 7:2 positive-to-negative ratio. To appreciate what they have accomplished and the job that we face, the next time you see a negative media report about us, substitute the word Jews for the word Mormons and ask yourself how Americans would react. Rage would justifiably descend on the offending reporter or commentator. So where's the fury when Mormons are the target?

For Comparison

What if these comments about Mormons in blogs and news releases . . .[3]	**. . . were made about Judaism and Jews instead?**
Mormonism is a Satanic cult!	Judaism is a Satanic cult!
If you vote for Mitt Romney, you are voting for Satan!	If you vote for Joseph Lieberman, you are voting for Satan!
Romney getting elected president will ultimately lead millions of souls to the eternal flames of hell!	Lieberman getting elected [vice] president will ultimately lead millions of souls to the eternal flames of hell!!!

On the bright side, it's becoming clear who our friends are. Catholics have a 53-33 favorable image of us, while Protestants have almost exactly the reverse, 32-53. The Gallup poll mentioned above showed virtually the same results – Catholics view us favorably, 56-31, while Protestants hold the opposite view, 36-52. The survey question that asked what people liked most and least about us (to be discussed momentarily) did not reveal any significant differences between the answers that Catholics and Protestants gave, so one is left to suppositions until the reasons can be probed more directly. My own theory has to do with religious security. Catholics see in Mormons a kindred religion – each has one person at the head of a hierarchical structure claiming to speak for God, promulgates uniform beliefs, and claims a line of authority back to Jesus Christ. We do not disturb their feelings of religious well-being. On the other hand, Protestants as a rule do not have as satisfying an explanation as to why they should be considered Christ's church – at least not one that every other person on the planet could not likewise claim. If the Catholics have the power Christ gave to Peter, they surely would not have passed it along to breakaway groups, and if Catholics do not have that power, the only way Protestants could get it would be through events such as we claim happened to Joseph Smith – the special authority was brought back by heavenly messengers. Shaky foundations sensitize one to the competition, which may be why anti-Mormon sermons over the pulpit seem to come more often than not from Protestants rather than Catholics.

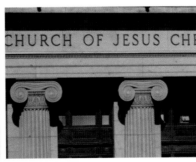

Images of Six Religions^

I will read you names of a few religious groups. For each one, please tell me whether you've heard of them, and if so, tell me whether your impression is strongly favorable, somewhat favorable, somewhat unfavorable, or very unfavorable.

	Strongly Favorable	Somewhat Favorable	Somewhat Unfavorable	Strongly Unfavorable	Heard of Only	Positive to Negative Ratio
Jews	20	47	12	8	12	3.4
Baptists	19	52	14	7	8	3.4
Catholics	15	43	21	14	7	1.9
Evangelicals	8	30	19	15	12	1.1
Mormons	5	32	26	23	12	0.8
Muslims	5	26	19	32	17	0.6

Groups

Highest groups giving Mormons favorable scores:

Catholics, 45-64s, pray often, upper-educated, moderates, Republicans, read Bible rarely

Highest groups giving Mormons unfavorable scores:

Read Bible daily, non-Christians, Baptists, Independents, very conservative, 35-44s, Protestants, 18-24s

It is also interesting to note that those who read the Bible daily are more likely to give us negative scores than those who rarely read the Bible.

^ Judged by those not of that faith.

The importance of expanding our circle of friends is demonstrated when we examine our image by the number of Mormons a person knows:

Image of Mormons

Positive

Negative

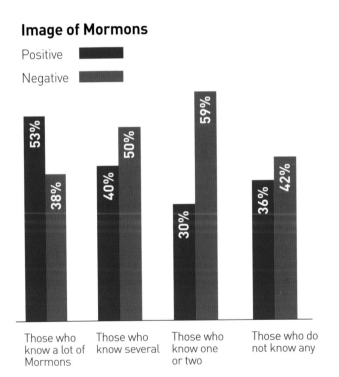

53% 38%

40% 50%

30% 59%

36% 42%

Those who know a lot of Mormons

Those who know several

Those who know one or two

Those who do not know any

One might have expected a stepwise pattern – that the more Mormons someone knows, the better the image. That the worst image of us comes from those who know only one or two Mormons is not difficult to understand if we consider the dynamics involved. When I conduct focus groups with participants from other faiths, I often ask them whether they have any Mormon friends, and to describe them. The first time I tried this question, I was taken aback when one young man replied, "I have a Mormon friend and we all like him because he can hold more beer than any of us."

I confess I was hoping for a description of someone a little higher on the food chain.

But then it occurred to me. It's human nature to choose friends who share one's interests, and an active member of the Church is not very likely to be found in a bar. While there are other venues where a suds gourmet could meet a strong member, it's not very likely because we all tend to associate with those holding similar values. Active members find their social needs filled by other active members, and less active members are more likely to know more people outside the Church.

So if a person knows only one member, the chances are high that the member will not be that active. If, however, he knows several or a lot of Mormons, our gregarious nature may be a factor: when a person meets an active member, and they hit it off, the chances are very good that this person will soon meet more active members. The moral: the sooner someone gets to know more than one member, the greater the probability that our image will improve.

First Impression Images

Part of the national sample (N=250) was asked standard
open-ended questions about what they like most and like least
about Mormons and Mormonism. The top categories are:

Things Americans Like Most about Mormons and Mormonism	
Category	**Sample Comments**
Family-oriented (21%)	"I like how they have a strong emphasis on family." **(Man, North Carolina)** "I like that the families seem to be close knit." **(Woman, North Dakota)** "Their views on the family; they are very family oriented." **(Man, California)** "They are family oriented and teach mostly based around the family." **(Woman, Washington State)**
Helpful (11%)	"Strong sense of community. They stick together no matter what." **(Man, Pennsylvania)** "They help each other and are always there for people who are not of their faith." **(Woman, Colorado)** "They are prepared for taking care of people in disasters." **(Woman, Missouri)**
Strong in their beliefs (11%)	"Their structure is something that they really try to live by." **(Man, Tennessee)** "Their dedication to their beliefs." **(Man, Washington State)** "They have the courage of their convictions." **(Woman, Florida)**
General positive (8%)	"They don't take their religion lightly." **(Man, Georgia)** "They actually participate in everything that has to do with their church." **(Man, Michigan)** "They have a more positive attitude." **(Man, California)**
Friendly, gentle, kind (6%)	"The Mormons I've met have always been very friendly." **(Woman, Texas)** "I find Mormons to be very nice people." **(Woman, Virginia)** "They are gentle people. They are cool people." **(Man, Texas)**
High moral standards (4%)	"I like their conservative moral beliefs the most." **(Man, Mississippi)** "I like most that they are moral and ethical because of their belief system." **(Man, New York)** "They have more character." **(Woman, Pennsylvania)**

Things Americans Like Least about Mormons and Mormonism

Category	Sample Comments
Polygamy (14%)	"Multiple marriage is wrong." **(Woman, Massachusetts)** "Their pledge to marry at an early age and that men can take on a 14-year-old girl." **(Man, Missouri)** "A woman can only go to heaven through marrying a man. There is no Trinity." **(Man, North Carolina)**
General negative (9%)	"I don't like their beliefs." **(Woman, South Carolina)** "I don't like Mormons and I don't care for their beliefs." **(Woman, Utah)** "They say we will become angels." **(Woman, Oregon)**
Doctrines in general (6%)	"They think they are going to be God some day." **(Man, Oregon)** "Their doctrine differentiates [sic] greatly from the fundamentals that Christ teaches." **(Man, New Jersey)** "Their belief that you have to work your way to go to heaven." **(Man, Texas)**
Beliefs about Jesus (5%)	"They are not Christian. They don't believe Jesus is the Son of God." **(Woman, Tennessee)** "They do not hold Jesus as the Messiah or a prophet, but as equal to other beings." **(Woman, Alabama)** "They are absolutely wrong about salvation and Jesus Christ." **(Man, Arkansas)**
Joseph Smith & Mormon history (4%)	"They have a whole concept of how some guy had golden plates. They sound like they believe in magic." **(Woman, Georgia)** "It's a made-up religion from Mr. Smith, and it keeps changing within the current times." **(Woman, Colorado)**
Status of women (4%)	"I don't like their historical beliefs about women and African Americans." **(Man, Maryland)** "What I like least is the woman's role." **(Woman, Delaware)** "I do not like their treatment of women. They lack equality, not only in the home, but also in their church." **(Woman, Vermont)**
Exclusionary (4%)	"I dislike the locking of everyone else out." **(Man, Connecticut)** "They isolate themselves. They're secretive." **(Man, North Carolina)** "I like least that they won't allow everyone to participate in their religion." **(Man, Ohio)**

If it were possible to have a single-sided image, the positives that people point out about us would be the perfect components. We preach the importance of the family – not only throughout eternity but also as the building block of civilization here on earth – and our fellow citizens recognize our commitment. We preach the need to reach out and help one another, and our sense of community is also recognized. Similarly, we teach dedication to Christ's teachings, generosity, and morality, and at least a few Americans are aware of these as well. Naturally, we cannot expect people to praise our theology, but sociologically speaking, many of the comments we received identified good things people recognize in us.

The problem is that our image has multiple facets, and the negatives about us reveal much misidentification and ignorance. Many answers of the "like least" variety indicate that people are confused about who is a Mormon. Media stories about polygamous sects in the Southwest are obviously contributing to this false impression. The Church is continually seeking to educate reporters and editors about the true nature of our religion, but even when people know that the LDS Church is not the same as the self-named fundamentalist groups, there remains a tendency to group both under one umbrella.

We are also hurt by false claims about our beliefs and our character traits. The February survey measured our image from another angle when interviewers asked a separate segment of the sample a right-brain question: "If Mormons were an animal, what animal would they be, and why?" A third of this sample could not wrap their minds around this unusual approach, and no animals broke into double digits, but consider the variety of interesting answers and the reasons for their choices:

If Mormons Were an Animal

Category	Sample Comments
Dogs (9%)	"A German shepherd. I was looking for something that was strong but capable of kindness." **(Woman, California)** "Labrador because some are loyal, strong, smart, and tolerant." **(Woman, Virginia)** "A golden retriever because they are smart and good." **(Woman, Indiana)**
Lambs / Sheep (6%)	"Sheep. They are harmless and they mean well. They follow a leader that they don't necessarily understand. Mormons are very devout and sheep are symbolic in the Bible." **(Woman, Kentucky)** "A lamb because they follow the flock and they are gentle." **(Woman, Colorado)** "A peaceful animal that is like a lamb." **(Woman, Alaska)**
Horses (5%)	"A horse because they are hard working, strong, and dependable, with a strong belief system." **(Woman, Missouri)** "They would be like a horse because of their intellect and sturdiness." **(Man, Maine)**
Cats (4%)	"A cat. They are nice to be around." **(Man, Pennsylvania)** "A cat because they are secretive and mean in their own way." **(Man, Iowa)**
Rabbits (4%)	"A rabbit because they are very family oriented, and most of them have a lot of children." **(Woman, Arizona)** "Rabbits because they stay to themselves and do their own thing." **(Woman, New Hampshire)**

If Mormons Were an Animal

Category	Sample Comments
Birds (4%)	"An eagle because they are strong and proud." **(Woman, Oklahoma)** "A dove because they are very quiet, peaceful people." **(Woman, New York)**
Lions / Tigers (4%)	"A large cat like a lion or a tiger because they can be nurturing as well as protect themselves, but also hunt if they need to." **(Man, California)** "Lions because they are strong in their beliefs. They have strong family beliefs. They are close to their family." **(Woman, Illinois)**
Bears (3%)	"The Mormons are like teddy bears. I don't think that they are aggressive or out to take over the world. They are kind, nice people." **(Woman, Illinois)** "A bear. They can get irate over something if something is threatening them. Otherwise, they generally leave people alone." **(Woman, Texas)**
Foxes (2%)	"A fox because Mormons tend to be very controlled and well trained. Their instincts are very precise. They are indoctrinated and they follow what they are indoctrinated in. Foxes are shrewd, sly, and wise. I mean that in a respectful way." **(Man, Pennsylvania)**
Deer (2%)	"Mormons are deer; they are being targeted politically." **(Man, Minnesota)** "A deer. They are peaceful people and they have peaceful lives." **(Woman, West Virginia)**
Snakes (2%)	"A python. They tend to squeeze all humanity out of religion. Certain aspects of the religion hurt people." **(Man, Wyoming)**
Miscellaneous Positive	"Giraffes because they are strong in their beliefs and gentle, like a kind animal." **(Woman, New Jersey)** "A beaver because they are hard working and they do their missionary work. They also provide for the needy." **(Woman, North Carolina)** "A prairie dog. Something furry, warm, and fuzzy." **(Woman, New Mexico)**
Miscellaneous Negative	"A ram because they force their religion on others." **(Man, North Carolina)** "A lemming. They're slightly misguided and they follow everything without thinking." **(Woman, Colorado)** "A coyote because I think they are scavengers." **(Man, Idaho)**

Many answers compared us to domesticated animals (horses, dogs, cats, sheep), which are indicators of the image we would like people to have of us – that we are hard working, loyal, gentle, smart, kind, and peaceful. Animals of strength and speed, of which we have a modest share, are generally considered positive associations, but this depends on whether the respondent chooses to view lions and eagles, for example, as regal or as predators.

There were extreme answers as well. The worst animals to be associated with are snakes, skunks, rats, and hyenas, of which we have a few mentions. But even the positive teddy bear answer from the woman in Illinois suggests a problem in that she felt the need to challenge something she had obviously heard – that Mormons are aggressive and out to take over the world.

Fortunately, people in this particular measure, even some who had previously stated in the name-impressions question that they have an unfavorable image of us, chose to emphasize the positive elements of our image.

Some people hold quasi-contradictory images of us, or at least recognize dual sides of our image in a yes-but format, a pattern that also appears in the word associations discussed in the next segment. Note answers such as these:

Summary of Animal Answers

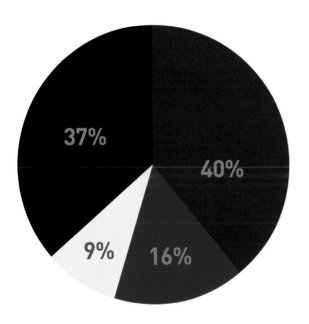

 **40%** positive

16% negative

9% neutral

 **37%** could not give an answer

"Let's go with a fox. They look sharp on the outside, but they are pretty darn sneaky – there is a different message going on – in the inside." **(Woman, Oregon)**

"A zebra because they have two different sides to them." **(Man, Alabama)**

"They would be a koala bear because they are very strong and very sensitive at the same time. They're very friendly, but don't cross them." **(Woman, New York)**

"They would be a bear. A bear is the best of both worlds. They can live in a city, and they can be aggressive when they want to be." **(Man, Virginia)**

"I believe they would be a rhinoceros because they stand firm and strong in their beliefs, but they are short-sighted." **(Man, Michigan)**

"The cat because they do not always show their true selves. They sit like angels, but can be hypocritical." **(Man, Texas)**

"They would be baboons. Like baboons, they have very strong family units. They have certain rituals which they follow that do not exist in other animal kingdoms." **(Man, Colorado)**

"A bear. They can get irate over something if something is threatening them. Otherwise, they generally leave people alone." **(Woman, Texas)**

Word Associations: The Church

The national sample was divided into four 250-respondent groups, and each was read a dozen or so words or phrases. Two groups were asked whether or not they felt each word or phrase described the Mormon Church, and the other two groups whether it described Mormons in general. Here are the percentages of people outside of our faith who believe a word or phrase describes the Mormon Church as an institution:

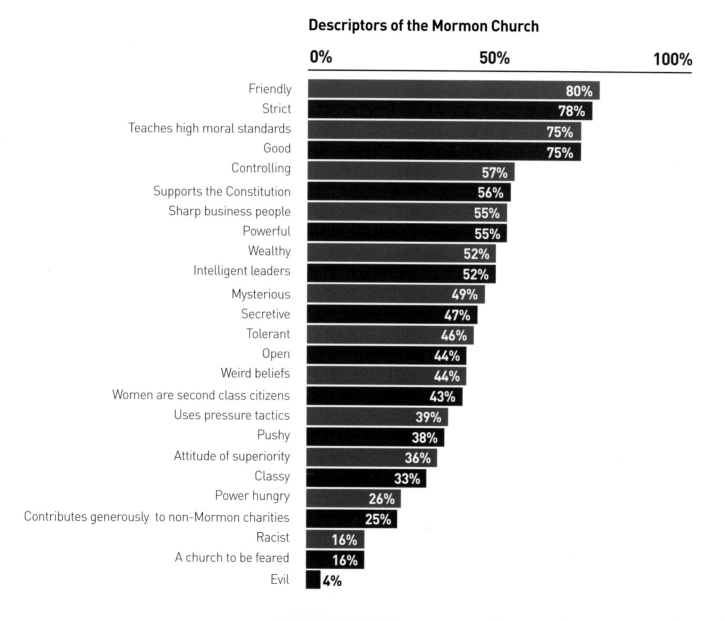

Descriptors of the Mormon Church

Descriptor	Percentage
Friendly	80%
Strict	78%
Teaches high moral standards	75%
Good	75%
Controlling	57%
Supports the Constitution	56%
Sharp business people	55%
Powerful	55%
Wealthy	52%
Intelligent leaders	52%
Mysterious	49%
Secretive	47%
Tolerant	46%
Open	44%
Weird beliefs	44%
Women are second class citizens	43%
Uses pressure tactics	39%
Pushy	38%
Attitude of superiority	36%
Classy	33%
Power hungry	26%
Contributes generously to non-Mormon charities	25%
Racist	16%
A church to be feared	16%
Evil	4%

The Church as an institution receives a few good marks, but I had hoped for more traits that score in the 80-90% range. Being good, for example, is such an intrinsic trait common to organizations that seek to do good that it should be a no-brainer to give a church, any church, better than a 75% score.

Of greater concern, given what we will discuss later about power and agendas, is that our perceived support of the Constitution is only a 56, especially in light of our belief that it is an inspired, even sacred, document from God establishing a base of operations for the restored Church. Unless more people come to understand our devotion to the Constitution, fears about our growth and the untruths related to our supposed political agenda will continue to spread, two indications of which are the 57% who describe the Church as controlling and the 55% who describe it as powerful.

The reasons for certain scores are easy to surmise. The low score on openness (44%) and a relatively high score on being secretive (47%) are plausibly driven by perceptions about temple worship. Similarly, descriptions of the Church as controlling or mysterious are not out-and-out negatives inasmuch as any hierarchical organization will be known for its controls, and being mysterious can even be considered a godly trait, as we know He moves in such ways. But when these scores are considered in light of the high scores on the definitely negative traits, they reflect a negative sheen as well. Fortunately, no truly negative descriptors of the Church garner majority agreement, but a few relatively high scores definitely trigger concerns:

- Weird beliefs   44
- Women are second-class citizens   43
- Uses pressure tactics   39
- Pushy   38
- Attitude of superiority   36

Tie these together with a touch of power hunger (26) and a residue of racism (16), and it becomes easier to understand why a segment of Americans feels justified in not listening to us explain who we are and what we believe. It is not yet a red flag, but definitely a yellow one.

The low 25% score on "contributes generously to non-Mormon charities" is also disturbing. The Church received fairly good publicity regarding its relief efforts in the wake of Katrina and the December 2004 tsunami in south Asia, but the resulting positive image apparently did not stick. It is understandable that a third of Americans do not know about the Church's significant welfare programs that work with relief agencies from other religions and non-profit groups to alleviate suffering, but among those who are willing to render a judgment about our humanitarianism, more people, by a 3:2 margin, would not describe the Church as an institution that contributes generously to non-Mormon charities. Sometimes it's hard to get a break.

Word Associations: The Members

We members are viewed more positively than the institution of the Church as a whole, perhaps because it is easier to describe people than organizations. But at a deeper level, it is not unusual for someone to think highly of a Mormon friend without that sentiment extending to the Church. This clearly came through in the rank-ordering of descriptive words and phrases in that all of the positive descriptions of Mormons in general achieved a majority agreement, and all of the negatives less than a majority, something that was not fully the case with the descriptors of the Church we just examined.

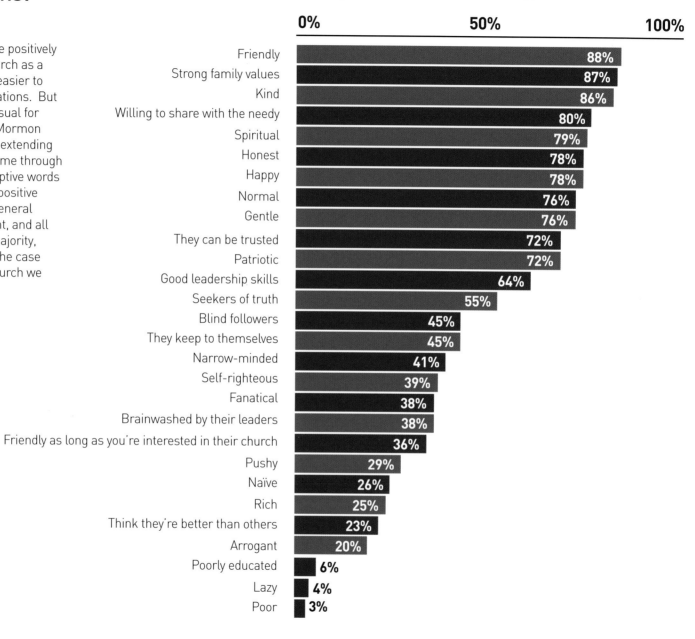

Descriptors of Mormons in General

Descriptor	Percentage
Friendly	88%
Strong family values	87%
Kind	86%
Willing to share with the needy	80%
Spiritual	79%
Honest	78%
Happy	78%
Normal	76%
Gentle	76%
They can be trusted	72%
Patriotic	72%
Good leadership skills	64%
Seekers of truth	55%
Blind followers	45%
They keep to themselves	45%
Narrow-minded	41%
Self-righteous	39%
Fanatical	38%
Brainwashed by their leaders	38%
Friendly as long as you're interested in their church	36%
Pushy	29%
Naïve	26%
Rich	25%
Think they're better than others	23%
Arrogant	20%
Poorly educated	6%
Lazy	4%
Poor	3%

The results speak well of our members in general. Scores in the 80s on such traits as friendly, strong family values, kind, and willing to share with the needy are solid tributes to the kinds of people in the Church. The traits that attracted agreement in the 70s evidence the same tone: spiritual, honest, happy, normal, gentle, trustworthy, and patriotic. In fact, from a later question, 84% think we're nice people rather than wacky (10%), even though 34% think we have irrational beliefs. There's a lot to be pleased with.

But we see a distinct negative side as well. Though a majority of Americans do not ascribe to us any of the negative traits tested, between 38% and 45% are willing to describe us as blind followers, insular, narrow-minded, self-righteous, fanatical, and brainwashed by our leaders. When asked whether they view our missionaries as teachers or salesmen, 49% said salesmen and 34% said teachers. This mix of perceptions leads me to the following observations:

- Americans compliment us the most on risk-free traits. A person risks little, if any, of his own religious security by saying that Mormons are kind, friendly, have strong families, etc.

- People are not nearly as positive about us when asked if they would describe us as seekers of truth. Only 55% are willing to grant us this central, Christian characteristic. Perhaps they feel they are not being loyal to their own beliefs if they so label people with whom they have strong doctrinal differences – a classic case of damning with faint praise.

- The collection of negatives they are willing to apply to us suggests that they view us as a growing threat. "Narrow-minded, brainwashed fanatics" does not describe harmless couch potatoes. That they do not brand us as poor, lazy, or poorly educated further reinforces this, and in fact, we might be seen as less of a threat if those were our characteristics.

So who are the "they" who hold these negative attitudes about us – either of the Church as an institution or of Mormons in general?

Those with above-average perceptions of the Church as mysterious, secretive, weird, pushy, power hungry, etc. are a mixed bag:

- 45-54 year olds, but also a mix of younger groups

- Liberals, especially the very liberal

- Daily blog readers

- Read Bible rarely or never

- Medium or low education

- Know an active Mormon

- Baptists and Evangelicals

- No religious affiliation

What this suggests is that certain blogs may be the source of much misinformation about the Church as an institution, especially for those on the outskirts of the religious world who may have a liberal worldview. That Baptists and evangelicals are also higher than average in their negative assessment of the Church should come as no surprise.

As for the traits of members, those with above-average perceptions of Mormons in general as brainwashed, fanatical, naïve, blind followers, narrow-minded, etc., are even more of a mixed bag, including opposite groups:

- The very liberal and the very conservative
- Non-Christians and the unaffiliated
- Residents in the Northeast
- Baptists and Evangelicals
- Those who have changed religions
- Less than a high school education as well as college graduates
- Do not know any Mormons
- Those claiming high knowledge of LDS beliefs
- Divorced
- Minorities
- 25-34-year olds
- And even those who say they are curious about our religion

What this pattern indicates is that **negative perceptions of us as a people can come from any segment of society, at any point along a spectrum**.

As we try to understand the reasons for the unfavorable side of our image, it is instructive to look at the word-association scores of those who hold an unfavorable impression of us. Whether the word or phrase was applied to the Church as an institution or to us as Mormons, here are the perceived traits for which our detractors – those who have a somewhat or strongly unfavorable impression of us – give us scores that are significantly different from the average scores of the total non-LDS population.

Detractors' Perceptions of Mormons

Trait	Total Non-LDS Score	Score of Our Detractors	Difference
Naïve	26	46	+20
Brainwashed	38	57	+19
Weird beliefs	44	63	+19
Fanatical	38	56	+18
Blind followers	45	62	+17
Narrow-minded	41	55	+14
Pushy	38	49	+11
Mysterious	49	60	+11
Controlling	57	69	+11
Can be trusted	72	61	-11
Seekers of truth	55	44	-11
Good	75	62	-13
Tolerant	46	28	-18

These patterns do not necessarily indicate a causal arrow – we do not know whether respondents' perceptions of traits preceded their formation of the general image assessment or vice versa – but they do indicate a strong correlation and are clear indications of what is bothering our detractors.

One would expect detractors to give us higher negative and lower positive scores than the average American, but the starker profile that emerges is of a type: that we are naïve, brainwashed, weird, fanatical, narrow-minded, and blind followers. Are these perceptions merely benign observations to be shrugged off as ignorance, or might they be early indicators of fear – a significant fear that we Mormons are a malleable and unthinking lot that will do whatever our leaders ask us to do? If the latter, it would not take much of a leap to compare us with groups that are dangerous. At a minimum, **these perceptions suggest an underlying unease or concern about us** among a not-insignificant portion of the U.S. population.

We may be puzzled as to why we have a multi-faceted unfavorable image, but it is what it is, and we must work with the world's perceptions as they are. We are unlikely to achieve a 90% favorable image this side of the Millennium, but I'm convinced that we can raise favorable impressions of us from the 30s into the 60s as individual members in one-to-one conversations correct the misperceptions and distortions that are now common about us.

Knowledge about Mormonism

 It's not what he doesn't know that bothers me, it's what he knows for sure that just ain't so.

- Will Rogers

While 98% of our fellow citizens have heard of Mormons, their knowledge about us as a people and as a church **ranges from accurate to appalling**. But we should not be too hard on our fellow citizens if they do not know a lot about Mormonism. First of all, we have been less than clear in conveying basic information about us. As Elder M. Russell Ballard noted, "The many misunderstandings and false information about the Church are somewhat our own fault for not clearly explaining who we are and what we believe."[4]

And second, our countrymen may not be that well acquainted with any religion, let alone ours. Whereas Americans in the 19th and well into the 20th centuries were quite well versed in the Bible and familiar enough with the various denominations to discuss intelligently their differences, that is not the case today.

Stephen Prothero, chair of the religion department at Boston University, tells of a visiting professor from Austria observing that American undergraduates are very religious but know next to nothing about religion, whereas European students know religious facts (thanks to compulsory religious education) but wouldn't be caught dead going to church. Prothero continues in his book Religious Literacy:

> Americans are both deeply religious and profoundly ignorant about religion. They are Protestants who can't name the four Gospels, Catholics who can't name the seven sacraments, and Jews who can't name the five books of Moses. Atheists may be as rare in America as Jesus-loving politicians are in Europe, but here faith is almost entirely devoid of content. One of the most religious countries on earth is also a nation of religious illiterates.[5]

He then cites these facts from various surveys:[6]

- Only half of American adults can name even one of the four Gospels.
- Most Americans cannot name the first book of the Bible.
- Only one-third know that Jesus delivered the Sermon on the Mount.
- A majority of Americans wrongly believe that the Bible says that Jesus was born in Jerusalem.
- When asked whether the New Testament book of Acts is in the Old Testament, one quarter of Americans say yes. More than a third say they don't know.
- Teachers of religion are fives times more likely to say Bible knowledge is decreasing than to say that it is increasing.
- Ten percent of Americans believe that Joan of Arc was Noah's wife.

Though we swim in an ocean of religious illiterates, there are, nonetheless, many Americans who are conscientious about their religious duties. My survey found that …

- 68% of all Americans pray at least several times a week
- 44% attend religious services every or almost every week
- 30% read the Bible daily or several times a week

With that as backdrop, let's look at the specific knowledge people have of us.

General Knowledge

On a zero-to-ten scale measuring how much people claim to know about Mormons and their beliefs . . .

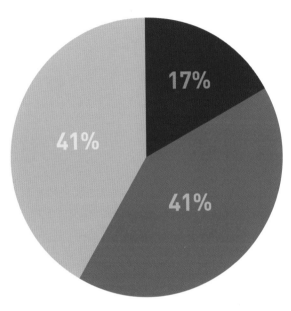

■ **17%** of non-LDS Americans claim to know a lot (8-10 on the scale)

■ **41%** claim middle-range knowledge (5-7)

■ **41%** claim their knowledge is in the lowest range (0-4)

If we eliminate those of the particular religion being asked about, then knowledge of Mormons and their beliefs in comparison to knowledge of Catholics, Evangelicals, and Muslims, just to select three differing comparison points, is as follows:

	High	Medium	Low
Mormons	17	41	41
Catholics	34	42	24
Evangelicals	16	32	49
Muslims	15	30	55

There are fewer people who claim low knowledge of us than claim low knowledge of Evangelicals by eight percentage points (49% vs 41%), but 33% of non-Evangelicals hold an unfavorable image of Evangelicals, whereas 49% of non-Mormons give Mormons an unfavorable rating, a 16-point gap. This suggests that lack of knowledge is not the sole correlation with unfavorable impressions. Something else is going on and it necessarily relates to the quality of the knowledge people think they have of us, especially as it relates to stories they may have heard that upset them. As will become clear, **our image is being driven by both an ignorance factor and a fear factor.**

Main Claim

One of the most interesting findings in the national study was that so few people know the central claim of Mormonism, a claim so basic that it is even implied in the formal name of the Church. They were asked: "To the best of your understanding, what is the main claim of Mormonism?" No choices were given, but people could state their understanding in whatever words they wanted. If they mentioned the words *restoration*, *re-established*, *original church*, or anything synonymous, we gave them credit for a correct answer. In this whole nation where missionaries have surely knocked on every door at one time or another, and which has been penetrated by many of our ads, **only 14% could tell the interviewers the main claim of Mormonism** – an 86% ignorance factor.

Similarly, in the summer of 2007, the Pew Forum on Religion and Public Life conducted a national survey[7] and asked respondents what one word best describes their impression of the Mormon religion. Not one person suggested the words *restored*, *original*, *re-established* or any synonymous expression. Less than 1%, probably our own members, said the word *true*. The major message we've been trying to send the world does not pop up in a simple word-association exercise about us.

It may come as a surprise to some, **but the world is not paying as much attention to us as we may think.**

> The major claim of Mormonism – the restoration, be it expressed in whatever synonymous words – has not penetrated the public's collective consciousness.

Groups

Highest groups aware of our claim, unaided:

Moderates, 18-34, upper-income, West, Republicans, men

Interviewers later read our claim to the respondents, half hearing
the simplest form and the other half a more extensive version.
They were then asked whether they could recall ever having heard it:

	Yes
Have you ever heard that Mormons claim to be the re-established original Christian church?	*29%*
Mormons say that Christ organized a church when He was on the earth. They say that men changed it. They say that it has been brought back. In other words, Mormons believe that theirs is the original Christian church that has been re-established by heavenly messengers. Have you ever heard that this is what Mormons claim?	*28%*

It is quite revealing that more than four out of five non-LDS
Americans (84%) have seen our ads, been given our literature,
and/or had missionaries approach them, **yet less than three
out of ten can recall what we have been trying to tell the world
for almost 180 years,** even when it is read to them.

Is it any wonder that there is so much confusion about us?

Groups

Highest groups aware of our claim, aided:

Post-grads, divorced, above $50K income, pray and
read Bible daily, unfavorable image of Mormons,
some college and college grads, 55-64, very liberal,
West, Republicans

Specific Knowledge

Dr. Henry Eyring, father of President Henry B. Eyring of the First Presidency, taught chemistry at Princeton for 15 years, many of which overlapped with Albert Einstein's time on campus, thus affording him opportunities to trade insights with the famous physicist. According to Dr. Eyring, after one such discussion, ". . . We walked out into what had been a rose garden, but in wartime had been replanted as a victory garden. Now, I'm a farmer from Pima [Arizona], so I guessed what the crop was, but I didn't know whether Einstein knew or not. So I picked up a plant and asked him what it was. He didn't know. We walked about a hundred yards to where the gardener was sitting on his wheelbarrow. As I walked by, I asked him what it was. He said, 'They're soybeans.'"[8]

Professor Eyring told this story many times over his years as a teacher and regaled people with the punch line they quickly anticipated – that Einstein was a brilliant man, but he didn't know beans.

We live in a world of ever-quickening advancement in all fields of knowledge. Even so, many people, like Einstein, may have advanced knowledge about many things, but they don't know beans about the Church.

Consider the knowledge findings shown below, again calculated on the non-LDS part of the sample:

Knowledge of Mormonism

For each of the following questions, please tell me whether you feel the best answer is . . .
definitely yes, probably yes, probably no, or definitely no. To the best of your knowledge . . .*

	Definitely Yes	Probably Yes	Probably No	Definitely No	Don't Know
Do Mormons believe in the Bible?	**33**	**39**	11	6	11
Are Mormons Christians?	**23**	**49**	10	11	8
Are Mormons a cult?	13	16	**28**	**33**	10
Do you have to be personally invited before you can attend a Mormon worship service?	9	15	**27**	**15**	34
Do Mormons practice polygamy?	14	25	**26**	**15**	21
Do Mormons worship Joseph Smith?	10	19	**22**	**16**	33

*Correct answers are in bold.

We have made a little progress in recent months in terms of being recognized as Christians, but note the tentativeness of the answers. Only one out of four is definitely sure that we are Christians, two out of four are only probably sure, and another one in four says that we are not or that they don't know. In other words, three-fourths of our nation's people do not know the true answer for certain.

We do better on perceptions that we believe the Bible, **but 85% of the nation are not sure that we do not practice polygamy**. Though we may think the polygamy issue was settled over a century ago, it is still the number one association people have when they hear the word *Mormon*. In a Gallup poll asking for free association with the word *Mormon* and without offering any choices, 18% spontaneously said *polygamy*, the highest single category.[9]

Our stake presents an annual Christmas nativity exhibit that includes live musical performances. A friend was ushering one year, standing by a huge Christmas tree surrounded by 700 beautifully displayed nativity sets as a choir sang "O Little Town of Bethlehem," when a lady came up to her and asked, "Pardon me, but are you Mormons Christians?"

Few people know, and are sure that they know, the correct answer about the six beliefs and practices we asked about. That being the case, everyone else is at least a little uncertain. Note this uncertainty level in the table below.

Belief Perceptions and Uncertainty Levels

	Definitely Correct	Uncertainty Level
Worship services	15	85
Polygamy	15	85
Joseph Smith	16	84
Christians	23	77
The Bible	33	67
A cult	33	67

A majority lean toward believing that we are Christians, that we believe the Bible, and that we are not a cult, but the uncertainty level is still huge. This indicates that **they have not received information they feel they can fully trust.** Consider:

- Of the 71% who have seen our TV ads, the uncertainty factor on the six knowledge questions above ranges from...   62% to 81%

- Of the 27% who have had a substantial conversation with a member, the uncertainty factor ranges from...   55% to 71%

- Of the 3% who have had an email conversation with a Mormon friend, the uncertainty factor ranges from...   37% to 64%

This means that **while our media vehicles are arriving, our message is not sticking**. But when a person has had a substantial conversation with a member, the confusion decreases because …

… we tend to trust information given to us by a friend more than we do information we receive through the media, and …

… we tend to remember information we trust.

The uncertainty drops further when there is an email conversation, an effective and comfortable mode of communication that few of us have taken advantage of to provide information about our religion.

So why don't people know beans about us? **Because we members have not told them** in words they understand.

Belief Comparisons

One of the most interesting measures in the study involved the comparison of respondents' own beliefs with what they believe Mormons believe. I chose eight doctrinal teachings, the first four of which were presented to respondents no matter their religion, while the last four in the series were only presented to non-Mormon Christians. Here are the side-by-side comparisons (LDS doctrine is in bold):

Personal Belief Systems Compared to Perceptions of Mormon Beliefs			
Do (you) *(Mormons)* believe...	**Personal Belief System**	**Perception of Mormon Belief**	**Observations**
God is a caring God who has a plan for us and helps us individually *or* *God is a distant and aloof God who does not intervene in our lives?*	85 8	71 7	This overwhelming belief that God is caring and interested in us individually runs counter to the cynicism of the world that often considers God to be distant and unlikely to intervene in our lives. A Baylor study in 2005-2006 identified four categories from answers to a mail-out poll: an Authoritarian God (31%), a Benevolent God (23%), a Critical God (16%), and a Distant God (24%).[10] When given the choices the Lawrence Research survey presented, however, people want to believe that God is our Father, with all the positive traits that appellation implies. This suggests that our work to explain Heavenly Father's plan should fall on receptive ears.
We live after death *or* *This life is all there is?*	82 13	57 10	Although most respondents chose the correct answer here, it is disappointing that the 57% is so low. Why do people know so little about us that they did not even guess the simplest of all religious beliefs? A religion without a belief in life after death is all but a contradiction in terms.
Our life began at birth *or* ***We lived with God before coming to the earth?***	61 28	19 31	Our belief in the pre-earthly existence of man is a unique and comforting doctrine that arouses no strong opposition, such as found, for example, with the doctrine of grace. Although we would prefer to see a higher number, the 28% who already believe that we lived with God before coming to the earth may be having a difficult time finding a religion that so teaches. Women, Catholics, and singles are above average in believing this.
There can be only one true religion *or* *There are many true religions?*	30 59	57 17	Non-LDS Americans have a pretty good idea that we differ with them on the concept of a true religion. The "many true religions" position – driven by Protestant denominations – has grown significantly since the days when nearly every church was arguing that it alone was the true representative of God on earth.

The following questions about personal belief systems were asked only of Christians, and perceptions of Mormon beliefs were gathered only from non-LDS Christians:			
Do (you) *(Mormons)* believe...	Personal Belief System	Perception of Mormon Belief	Observations
God, Jesus Christ, and the Holy Ghost are three separate Beings *or* *They are three Beings in one body or substance?*	24 71	27 23	If there is one doctrine on which half of all Americans should not be undecided about our position, this is it. But half of all Christians in America could not even take a guess. Equally troubling is that almost as many feel we believe the three-in-one creeds as feel that we believe the Godhead is composed of three separate Beings. We have not adequately conveyed to America this basic and central concept in our panoply of doctrines.
Did Jesus Christ organize a church during His ministry *or* *Was it organized by His followers after His crucifixion?*	34 62	16 36	If Christians are asked – yes or no – whether Christ organized a church when He was on the earth, 52% tend to believe He did. But if given a choice as to how this organization came about, the results are as shown to the left. Our position, so critical to an understanding of the apostasy and subsequent restoration, is known by only 16% of American Christians. People impute to us their own belief that the Church was organized by Christ's followers rather than by the Savior Himself.
Religious revelation is when God speaks to a person, such as Moses or Abraham, who then instructs people what God wants them to do. Do you/Mormons believe... *Religious revelation stopped with the death of Christ's apostles* *or* **Religious revelation is still possible today?**	 10 83	 10 57	America's collective personal belief system runs counter to the teachings of many pastors and ministers who deny that God speaks to prophets today. People hope for the possibility that such revelation exists and lean toward our teaching on this matter. In a nation where 75% pray at least once a week, and obviously do so expecting a result, it should be easy to explain that God can speak to us personally in answer to our prayers, and also to a prophet. The base is there to be built upon if we explain the difference between religious revelation of a personal nature and religious revelation intended for a people as a whole, for which a traditional prophet is necessary.
People are saved by the grace of Christ if they will only recognize Him as their Savior *or* **People are saved by the grace of Christ only after they do their best to live His commandments**	57 37	20 43	Our doctrine of Christ's grace – "that it is by grace that we are saved, after all we can do" – is a target that generates much distortion. That we believe a covenant is a two-way promise – that each party must fulfill certain obligations – has been twisted into the charge that we believe we can work our way into heaven. This false claim and red herring allows our critics to avoid having to defend their weak "no need for anything but lip service" approach to the doctrine of grace. But at least a plurality of other Christians understands our doctrinal position.

The summary below shows that a majority of Americans subscribe to the correct position on only three of the eight doctrines, but more people than not know or at least correctly guessed our position on seven of the eight. The problem is that substantial percentages of Americans had no opinion about our beliefs and were not even willing to hazard a guess.

Summary of Belief Comparisons				
Doctrine	Own Belief System Correct	Perceptions of Mormons Correct	Percent Correct Re Mormons	No Opinion Re Mormons
Nature of God	Yes	Yes	71	22
Life after death	Yes	Yes	57	33
Pre-mortal existence	No	Yes	31	50
One true church	No	Yes	57	26
Godhead	No	Yes	27	50
Organized the Church	No	No	16	48
Revelation	Yes	Yes	57	33
Grace	No	Yes	43	37

We have a good deal of work to do explaining the true nature of the Godhead and that Christ Himself organized His Church, two critical doctrinal issues if people are to be receptive to our teachings about the apostasy and the restoration.

Distortions flourish in a fact-poor atmosphere of uncertainty.

Reactions to Mormonism

 Mormonism is the only minority category where bias in America has deepened. [12]

- Robert Novak

In his book *Presidents* and *Prophets*, Michael K. Winder relates the story of President Ulysses S. Grant's visit to Utah in 1875. Grant, who had long been exposed to the anti-Mormon sentiments of the era, was the first U.S. president to visit the Mormon people:

"When a carriage took the presidential party from the railroad station to Grant's Salt Lake City hotel, South Temple Street was lined with throngs of white-clad children singing and throwing flowers before the President's carriage. Grant asked Governor Emery, 'Whose children are these?' When he learned that they were Mormon children, he reportedly murmured to himself, 'I have been deceived!'" [13]

Many people today, as then, are reacting to unsavory stereotypes spawned by ignorance. As they get to know more of us individually, reactions will be more along the lines that President Grant experienced.

Causes of Antagonism

One fourth of our sample (250 respondents) was asked this open-ended question:

Recent polls have found that as many as 45% of all Americans say they could not vote for a Mormon for president. Regardless of your own feelings on this matter and regardless of whom you may want as president, why do you feel there is such antagonism toward the Mormon religion in America today?

The perceived reasons for this antagonism follow:

Reasons for Antagonism Toward the Mormon Religion	
Category	**Sample Comments**
Ignorance (25%)	"There isn't enough information out there about them." **(Man, Iowa)** "They do not understand the religion and they become very fearful of what they do not understand. A lot of people feel they still have multiple wives." **(Woman, Connecticut)** "People are confused about Mormons. They are scared of them." **(Man, New York)** "A lot of it is that people aren't bothering to correct things." **(Woman, Florida)** "There is a lack of understanding and a lack of trust. The two coincide." **(Woman, Minnesota)**
Different Beliefs (9%)	"Their beliefs are contrary to the Bible in certain areas and that can cause antagonism." **(Man, Kentucky)** "They have some eccentric beliefs, like when you die you become a God." **(Man, Kansas)**
Polygamy (8%)	"People look at Mormons and think they are all into polygamy." **(Woman, Indiana)**
Not Christian (6%)	"It's because we basically were founded as a Christian nation. Mormons are outside that category and a different religion altogether." **(Man, Arkansas)**
Fear of Unknown (5%)	"People are afraid of what they don't know." **(Woman, New York)** "It is because they fear the unknown. They may have seen pictures of the founders and that frightens them." **(Woman, Georgia)**
Book of Mormon (5%)	"Their Bible is something that someone made up one day." **(Woman, South Dakota)** "They don't accept Mormons as true Christians because of the Book of Mormon." **(Woman, California)**
Joseph Smith (4%)	"It's based on a false prophet." **(Man, West Virginia)**
Negative History (4%)	"This may be because of their history of polygamy and racism." **(Woman, Washington State)**

Several things are contributing to the current antagonism toward us as Mormons, but the dominant factors are ignorance of our beliefs and the fear that is generated when people do not have the facts. Rumors begin easily in an atmosphere of ignorance, and that has been our burden since the 1820s, even in this age of quick access to information.

In fact, this abundance of information at the world's fingertips may work against us. In a slower-paced era, people could entertain most new ideas that came along. However, in our fast-paced day, when people are bombarded with stimuli, they resort to a form of triage to select which among an avalanche of ideas they will pay attention to. As a first step in this sorting process, they do not ask what positive attributes merit their attention as much as they ask whether there is anything in the idea that justifies rejecting it. In other words, they look for negatives first as a quick way to dispose of less worthy claims on their time. In our case as Mormons, **rumors and falsehoods precede us and tilt the judgment process against us** before we have a fair chance to explain who we are and what we believe.

Many people have already justified to themselves that they can safely ignore us, and changing this mindset, antagonistic or benign, requires the impact of mass media messages combined with the efforts of individual members in one-to-one conversations.

Political Factors

Mitt Romney's presidential candidacy smoked out of America's attitudinal underbrush a significant but previously hidden anti-Mormon sentiment.

In the spring of 2007, as Romney was campaigning for votes in Iowa, Jan Mickelson, a talk-radio host at WHO-AM in Des Moines, invited him for an interview. What started out as a friendly discussion "veered into a discussion of abortion and Mormonism, and the Republican presidential hopeful – eyes wide, arms waving – was clearly annoyed," according to the L.A. Times. Continuing the tussle during a commercial break, which was not heard at that time by the audience but recorded and later released by the station, Romney said, "Let me once again say I understand my faith better than you do," to which Mr. Mickelson replied, "Well, I'm not sure."

Think about that. The interviewer actually said, "Well, I'm not sure."[14]

Beyond the obvious arrogance of his claim to understand our religion better than a former stake president, the talk-show host was implying that Mormons are naïve and have been hoodwinked by their leaders, otherwise they would understand, as he supposedly does, what it is all about. How else can one explain why this self-identified Christian libertarian could claim to know more than an extremely intelligent, lifelong member who has served in multiple Church leadership positions?

And that is not an atypical example of the situation we face in the media.

By permission of Michael Ramirez and Creators Syndicate, Inc.

As America began its 2008 presidential primary season ...

- A Los Angeles Times/Bloomberg poll in the summer of 2006 revealed that 37% would not vote for a Mormon for president.[15]

- A Newsweek poll in December of 2006 found that 25% would not vote for a member of The Church of Jesus Christ of Latter-day Saints for president (compared to 8% who would not vote for a woman and 3% who would not vote for an African American), and 48% said they do not think America is ready to elect a Mormon president. [16]

- A Gallup poll in February of 2007 sweetened the qualifiers related to a Mormon candidate, but 24% said, nonetheless, that they would not vote for a generally well-qualified person for president that their own political party nominated if that person happened to be a Mormon.[17] This figure dropped to 17% in December, 2007, and happens to be

the same percentage who would not vote for a Mormon in 1967 when George Romney was a presidential candidate.[18]

- A January 2008 Wall Street Journal/NBC poll showed that 21% of all Americans would be very uncomfortable and 29% would have some reservations about a presidential candidate who is a Mormon.[19]

My national survey approached the political factor in Mormonism, specifically Mitt Romney's campaign (the poll was conducted approximately 10 days after Romney's suspension of his 2008 campaign for the presidency), from two angles. Our first approach was to measure the support for Romney across the whole political spectrum, so interviewers asked all Americans, even those who are not registered to vote, how they would have voted if they had been allowed to vote in a nationwide Republican primary.

Percentages in the teens or 20s may appear to some to be small enough to ignore. Their true significance emerges, however, when compared to what the number *should be*. That 24% would not vote for a well-qualified nominee from their own party if he happened to be a Mormon reveals substantial religious bias because the true number in a world free from such bias would be zero.

Vote Patterns for Romney by Key Group

Group	Romney First Choice	Romney Second Choice	No Romney Vote
All Americans	19	22	59
All non-LDS Americans	17	22	61
All Republican voters	29	26	58
All conservatives	23	23	54
All Republican conservatives	34	28	38
All who hold a favorable impression of Mormons	29	19	52
All who hold an unfavorable impression of Mormons	14	23	63
Republicans who hold a favorable impression of Mormons	39	27	34
Republicans who hold an unfavorable impression of Mormons	23	25	52
All non-LDS who know an active Mormon	21	23	56
All non-LDS who know a Mormon	19	22	59
All non-LDS who do not know a Mormon	14	23	63

As has been known for some time, Romney's fortunes, or lack thereof, correlate at least moderately with people's knowledge and impressions of Mormonism, and **thus suggest a pattern of religious bias**. No surprise there. What is interesting is examining vote differences between those holding favorable versus unfavorable impressions of Mormons and speculating what might have happened in the early 2008 presidential primaries if more people had known an active Mormon and our overall favorable-unfavorable image had been 49-37 instead of 37-49. The roughly two-percentage-point gain in Romney's vote would not have been enough to overturn the results in most of the primaries, but in contests in which momentum is the currency of the realm, Romney out-pointing McCain by 14 instead of by 12 in Iowa might have led to a tighter race in New Hampshire, which still would not have changed things in South Carolina, but might have had an influence on Florida. And so goes the "what if" game. Now, if our image had matched the 71-21 of the Baptists at the beginning of the election season. . . .

The second approach, which yielded additional evidence of anti-Mormon bias in the vote, came with a question known in the polling profession as a projective technique. Instead of asking a direct question about the respondent's own attitude, which answer would be softened with an eye to a socially acceptable posture, the projective technique asks the respondent to think about others he or she may know and then phrases the question of interest in terms of how the respondent thinks a specific group would answer, thus minimizing his or her image-protection posture. This technique is seen as a way of more accurately measuring the true bias, inasmuch as the respondent is likely to project his own attitudes on those he knows. Here is the way we phrased our question and the answers we received:

Think of the people who disapproved of Mitt Romney for president, which may include some people you personally know. Which of these choices comes closest to what you observed about people who disapproved of Romney?

They disapproved mainly because of his religion, but may have used another reason as their excuse   *27%*

Or

They disapproved mainly because of some other reason   *58%*

The 27% measured here is not guaranteed to be the true level of bias we would measure if all respondents had taken truth serum, but it is obviously higher than would be the case if the survey had asked people to admit bigotry in that they would not vote for Romney because of his religion. In all probability, the 27% is a conservative estimate.

Mormonism as the real reason to disapprove of Romney comes from men more than women, conservatives more than liberals, Republicans more than Democrats, and from the West and the South; Catholics are the least likely to suggest it. The bias among Republicans and conservatives, labels that also apply to the majority of Mormons, may be an outgrowth of backers of other candidates, wearing the same labels, searching for anything that would diminish Romney's candidacy.

In any case, **anti-Mormon sentiment** based on hearsay, rumor, and half-truths and fed by whisper campaigns, innuendoes posing as legitimate questions (hello, Mike Huckabee), and those who intentionally wish us harm, **is alive and well in America**, which I can confirm anecdotally from several eye-popping focus groups I have conducted over the years. **The Romney campaign simply brought it to the surface**. We should be prepared to see this bigotry more frequently employed, directly or behind the scenes, as our detractors deem expedient. The paucity of articles in the media disapproving of such religious bias toward us will only embolden them.

Authority and Fear

We Mormons are often criticized by leaders of other churches for claiming that our prophet receives modern-day revelation from God. They are free to dispute our claim, of course, and we welcome discussions about it. But they should know that sizeable numbers of Americans, including their own parishioners, believe that even leaders of latter-day-revelation-denying denominations receive such revelation. Interviewers posed this question to the national sample:

Leaders Who Speak For God

Religious revelation is when God speaks to a person, such as a leader of a religion, who then instructs people what God wants them to do. From what you understand, do _____ believe they have a leader who speaks for God?

	Yes	No	No Opinion
Catholics	69	23	7
Mormons	61	20	19
Muslims	51	27	22
Baptists	45	43	12
Methodists	37	41	22

One would expect people to be aware that Catholics believe their leader speaks for God, given the high media visibility of the pope. But I did not expect the relatively high numbers who believe that Protestant denominations such as Baptists and Methodists believe that they, too, have a leader who speaks for God. Survey research did not exist as an organized profession in the 1800s, but the generally accepted wisdom from that age is that ministers preached, and people believed, that the heavens were closed and that all revelation from God ceased with the death of Christ's apostles. That assertion is fraying in the 21st century.

This perception is especially important to the LDS image because at the same time some people are reassessing the idea of ongoing modern-day revelation, the charge of fanaticism is more frequently being leveled at those who believe their religious leaders speak for God. So my national survey checked out the perception among the non-LDS portion of the sample with this question:

Prophets and Fanaticism

If someone claims to have the authority to speak for God, does this almost always lead to fanaticism, or is it possible for someone to make that claim and not be a fanatic?

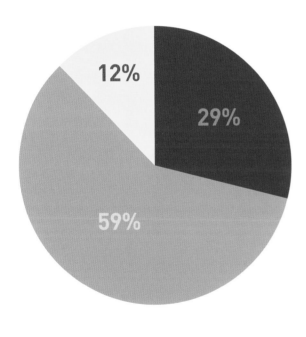

Some may see a bright side in this finding that three out of five people believe that someone can claim to have authority to speak for God and not be a fanatic. And we definitely would like to reach out and explain our message to them. But I believe **the problem is bigger than the opportunity**. There are very few religions that identify an individual by name as God's representative on earth – Catholics and Mormons being most prominent among them. Even Muslims, who claim that authority for their religion, split that authority among several leaders. Therefore, given this environment, when three in ten are inclined to believe such a claim almost always leads to fanaticism, we quickly come to people's minds if they have heard even a nominal amount of our doctrine regarding prophets.

As the nearby box of groups reveals, those highest in believing priesthood authority almost always leads to fanaticism tend to be secularists with few religious practices.

Groups
Highest groups believing authority to speak for God almost always leads to fanaticism: Non-Christians, never read Bible, unaffiliated with any religion, 25-34 year olds, very liberal, Democrats, pray rarely, post-grads, check blogs often

29% Almost always leads to fanaticism

59% Possible not to be a fanatic

12% No opinion

Now consider the definition of priesthood that every 12-year-old deacon is taught – that it is the authority to act in God's name. We mean this in the sense that ordinances performed here on earth will be valid on the other side. But those who only visualize God's actions in terms of reward for good and punishment for sin may easily and mistakenly assume that Mormons claim to have the authority to punish others.

As evidence, consider how many people believe we would be willing to use force if we had enough political power.

This and the previous finding indicate that we have a critical problem. Anything we do that could even remotely be interpreted as force will resonate among the 38% who already believe we are fanatic and the 49% who already hold negative impressions of us. How quickly certain people twist our claim of latter-day revelation into a fear of power, force, and fanaticism. In fact, the nearby box shows that those who can believe this about us include the young, the poorly educated, as well as people from outside organized religion, and those who are fairly conscientious about whatever religious habits they happen to possess.

Mormons and Political Power

If Mormons had enough political power, they would try to force people to convert.

Strongly agree

18%

Somewhat agree

19%

Somewhat disagree

20%

Strongly disagree

37%

Groups

Highest groups agreeing that if Mormons had enough political power, they would try to force people to convert:

Less than high school, 25-34 year olds, non-Christians, unaffiliated with any religion, minorities, women, attend weekly religious services, read Bible often, no votes cast for Romney

When we posed the same statement about Muslims, 68% agreed that they would try to force people to convert if they had enough political power. But just because Muslims are higher on the scale than we are does not solve our problem. And, in fact, almost half of all Americans believe that we can be just as fanatic as Muslims, and one in four strongly makes that connection.

Mormons, Muslims, and Fanaticism

Mormons can be just as fanatic as Muslims.

Strongly agree

25%

Somewhat agree

22%

Somewhat disagree

16%

Strongly disagree

21%

Of 170 pieces of data interviewers collected in my national survey, these results regarding fanaticism and force disturbed me the most. We may not presently be viewed as suspiciously as are Muslims (only 16% felt outright that we are a church to be feared), **but the potential fear of a fanatic application of political power is there**. Mix in the image scores already noted on such traits as being controlling, mysterious, secretive, pushy, blind followers, brainwashed, naïve, and narrow-minded, and we begin to appreciate the dimensions of a sizeable problem percolating just beneath the surface. Any pressure exuberant members may apply in seeking converts only feeds this fear, unjustified though it is.

Groups

Highest groups believing Mormons can be just as fanatical as Muslims:

Non-Christians, rarely pray or read the Bible, never attend religious services, very liberal, 25-44 year olds, college grads, single, changed religions, high school grads, Democrats, less than $50K income, read blogs daily

People do not know that the use of force runs contrary to everything we stand for – that force has no place in religion, ours or anyone else's. It may be the prerogative of governments, but never that of religions. That is so self-evident to us that we assume everyone must know it. But when so few people even know our claim to be the re-established original Church, and so many people still have distorted information about our other beliefs, how can we expect them to know our position on freedom, agency, and the right to choose, and that force is never an option in our religion?

Along with everything else, we must inform people that **voluntary choice is one of our core beliefs** – that God Himself so respected our right to choose that He allowed a third of His children to rebel and follow Lucifer. We differ not in the slightest from God's respect for individual choice and must reassure the world accordingly.

Anticipations

Related to the above fears are people's anticipations of what might happen if they undertook an investigation of the Church. Two versions of an investigation question were posed, one focusing on the missionaries and the other on the members:

Pressure or Mentor

If you decided to investigate the Mormon religion, do you feel Mormon (missionaries) (friends) would push you to make commitments and try to pressure you into joining, . . . or would they be mentors who would guide you in the study of their religion without pressure?

	Missionaries Would	Members Would
Would push and pressure	36	25
Would mentor and guide	42	50

That a fourth to a third of the people anticipate being pushed and pressured during any investigation of the Church, and that only half or less feel they would be guided in a mentored way, does not speak well of us.

Interest in Learning

Toward the end of the interview, another two-version question asked respondents to sum up their feelings about learning more about Mormonism:

At the end of the day, which of these three statements comes closest to your own feelings about Mormonism?

	From Friend	By Email
I would not mind learning more about Mormonism from the Mormon missionaries	3	8
I would not mind learning more about Mormonism if I could learn it from a friend without feeling any pressure to join	30	-
I would not mind learning more about Mormonism if I could learn it by email without feeling any pressure to join	-	16
I am not interested in learning anything about Mormonism*	63	71

Ten times as many people would be interested in learning more about us if a friend offers information in a way that does not cause them to feel any pressure to join than through traditional missionary work. As for learning about the Church by email, the 16% is a disappointing number, but the wording leaves unstated with whom the person would be communicating. Given that double that number would be willing to have a friend involved in the learning process, if I had specified that the email process would be guided by a friend, the percentage willing to learn under those conditions might well be substantially higher than the 30% measured above.

It is natural for us to want to know which groups are most open to our message. What the analysis uncovers, however, is that demographic and religious groups are all over the map when it comes to Mormonism.

Baptists, for example, are among the highest groups giving us an unfavorable image score, but are among the highest groups willing to learn about us from a friend. Republicans are the reverse – they give us a high image score but are among the highest groups uninterested in learning about us. Similarly, while one might expect very conservative Republicans to feel an affinity with Mormons, the Christian Right within that political segment tilts the group against us.

All of which reflects the oft-noted observation that there are few monolithic groups in today's society. We may narrow our target audiences to some degree, but in the last analysis, our image will be changed as we talk with people from all walks of life and all demographic groups.

Groups

Highest groups willing to learn about us from a friend:

18-34, liberals and moderates, singles, Baptists, those with at least some college education

Highest groups uninterested in learning about us:

Very conservative, high school graduates, divorced, minorities, seniors, Republicans, 35-54

* There are obviously additional ways of learning about our religion, so the 63% and 71% are not levels of absolute disinterest but only the percent who do not wish to learn through a personal contact with a member or missionary.

The six factors mentioned in the overview of this section boil down to two main problems – *ignorance*, which includes the polygamy factor, and *fears*, especially the power factor. While ignorance underpins much of America's image of us, **the greatest threat to our growth and well-being is the antagonism spawned by a variety of fears:**

- **Fear of change** – the fear that a new claim will require effort to prove or disprove, and the accompanying fear of possibly having to change and leave a comfort zone.

- **Fear of the new, the different, and the unfamiliar** – the fear fed by warped stories about a golden bible, temple ceremonies, multiple heavens, new words from Jesus, strange beliefs, etc.

- **Fear of undermined religious beliefs** – the fear that we may present evidence or reasoning that they cannot answer, or the fear of their own religion's inability to compete in the marketplace of ideas.

- **Fear of force** – the fear that somehow we Mormons will use whatever organizational abilities, wealth, and political power we may obtain to improperly influence, manipulate, and dominate the rest of society, or even use force in our quest for converts. This fear is even a factor in the investigation process as people may think, "If my Mormon friends push me to meet with the missionaries, and the missionaries push me to be baptized, what force will be applied after I join?"

We face serious challenges, but there is much we average members can do to help the honest and the open-minded resist the bigotry spawned by anti-Mormon agitators. **Softening such fear-driven antagonism will require new thinking, preparation, and effort.** The seven steps in the section that follows may provide you with useful ideas.

The Solution

Seven Steps Overview

 Bigotry is the disease of ignorance, of morbid minds. Enthusiasm of the free and buoyant, education, and free discussion are the antidotes of both.

- Thomas Jefferson

Although Church members can be proud of some of the findings in the national survey, too many results tip in a negative direction. Bigotry toward us is alive and well. The bottom-line fact that almost half of all Americans view us unfavorably indicates the severity of the problem, and the intensity of the negative feelings compels us to address this problem sooner rather than later.

A natural first thought is that we must engage ourselves in better missionary work, but admirable as that might be, the strong anti-Mormon sentiment uncovered by recent events suggests an additional approach. Whatever we are accustomed to doing in the way of member missionary work we should by all means continue doing. However, the image improvement to which it is now clear we must also devote ourselves is, though there are parallels, a different animal and thus requires different thinking.

- Whereas the goals of member missionary work are referrals and baptisms, the goals of image improvement are to correct misperceptions and provide accurate information about who Mormons are and what we believe.

- Whereas member missionary work involves numerical goals and statistical reports for management purposes, image repair remains informal and no one counts the number of times we plant new or more correct information in the minds of people with whom we talk.

- Whereas member missionary work aims to set up a formal teaching situation, image improvement takes place wherever we happen to be.

- Whereas member missionary work attempts to connect actions with outcomes (we contacted X number of people which led to Y number of baptisms Z days later), image building involves no such stimulus-response model.

To use a football analogy, improving our image involves many team members working independently to move the ball down the field a little at a time rather than a few members teaming up to score quickly on a long touchdown pass. Millions of members independently communicating truths about Mormons and Mormonism will ultimately effect a change in our image, although we may never know in this life the results of conversations we have with particular individuals with whom we happen to speak.

> Instead of a few doing a lot, we need many, each doing a little.

My youngest daughter, Lindsey, hoped for one of those inspirational "plane experiences" we hear about in Conference when she flew to Portland on business. A middle-aged man settled into his seat next to hers but said nothing. Lindsey felt impressed to take out the Young Women lesson she was preparing, pages of which she had copied and brought along in her carry-on, but not to say anything. The man soon glanced at the title, "Maintaining Chastity through Righteous Living," and commented, "That's interesting. What's it all about?" Thus began Lindsey's two-hour conversation with, it turned out, a concerned father of two teenage boys.

Lindsey was the first LDS person this Catholic from Kansas City had met, and she carried on a pleasant conversation in which she was able to share a few important facts about the Church, all without leaving her comfort zone. Did it lead to a referral? No, and that wasn't her goal. She was content to leave him with a few thought-generating observations. And when he meets the next member of the Church, and the next after that, if each adds some fact or impression to his mental Mormonism file, and if he's one of the Lord's sheep, he will eventually check out the Church.

> When the Savior instructed us to cast our bread upon the waters, He did not indicate when the results of our efforts would be revealed to us.

To improve our image, the objective, in a nutshell, is for more members of the Church to become individually known by more people, and for more of us to state facts in casual, friendly one-to-one conversations supporting the oft-quoted principle that it takes three to five stimuli to solidify an impression. Elder M. Russell Ballard gave us a guideline for such informal conversations in his October 2007 General Conference address, suggesting that we must all accept a greater responsibility to advance the public perception of the Church:

Sometimes people just want to know what the Church is. Those who are curious in this general way deserve clear and accurate information that comes directly from those of us who are members so they do not have to rely on the incomplete answers, half-truths, or false statements that may come from the media or other outside voices.[20]

So how do we explain who we are and what we believe? I have divided our task into seven steps.

The first three steps are preparatory, **how we change ourselves**. We will discuss how to break old ways of thinking, how to harness the power of simplification, and how to prepare for natural and comfortable conversations that touch upon religion:

Step 1: Think new

The world is changing and we must break old habits if we are to reach honest men and women who are currently unaware of our message or are blinded by the ignorance or craftiness of men. This means we must leave our fears, guilt, and vulnerability to pressure behind, think empathetically, and redefine what we consider success in conversing with those of other faiths.

Step 2: Think simple

A simple model for understanding where people stand, simple speech, and simple Golden Rule behavior give us a game plan to correct distortions and reach the open minded.

Step 3: Prepare the stage

Winston Churchill once excused himself from a dinner party saying he had to "practice [his] impromptus" for a speech the next day in the House of Commons. We, likewise, must prepare our impromptus in the form of facts we can casually drop into conversations. We further prepare when we thoughtfully observe what's going on in society and become more active in our communities.

The fourth step addresses **how we change the wary into the accepting**. It offers the greatest potential for changing our image with the most people.

Step 4: Have natural conversations

In any society, things get done by those who show up and speak up, and we members simply have not put enough facts about us on the public table. I will explain how we can do this without leaving our comfort zones. Merely stating a few pertinent facts will change our image, and we will have been successful even if our listeners show no further interest at the time.

The fifth and sixth steps explain **how we change the accepting into the defending** as we give friends and acquaintances a better understanding of why we believe and worship as we do.

Step 5: Expand the vision

As our facts and claims shake people's previous assumptions, we use contrast and reframing techniques to open and broaden their perspectives. People who understand us at a deeper level will be more likely to defend us in conversations where no member is present.

Step 6: Use technology

The written word facilitates comfortable soul-to-soul communication and helps people become not only our personal friends, but also friends of the Church. And we can accomplish this with the click of a mouse from our safe harbors.

Of course, the ultimate improvement in our image occurs when people join the Church. As additional survey results will later demonstrate, around 5% of all Americans could see themselves seriously investigating our religion. If only half of those so inclined actually join, we would double our membership in the nation and thus double the opportunity for others to get to know a member of the Church. Therefore, the last of the seven image-improvement steps explains **how we help interest become a testimony**.

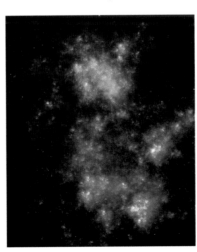

Step 7: Guide patiently

If our friends change their image of us and want to learn more, gentle mentoring is the key to fruitful investigation. I will explain how to cultivate the characteristics of gentle mentorship and how to help interested friends take control of the investigation process so that on joining, they will not feel they are visitors in someone else's church, but that they truly belong.

Think New

 The significant problems we face cannot be solved at the same level of thinking we were at when we created them.

- Albert Einstein

Changing the world's opinions of
Mormonism begins with changing the
applicable paradigm within which we
Mormons operate.

A paradigm is a model or pattern of how things relate to one another. In the following chapters we will consider new paradigms to use as we interact with those of other faiths. Whatever the reasons, our actions or lack thereof have contributed to a schizophrenic image – being a friendly, kind, honest people with strong family values and high moral standards on the one hand, and being a controlling, secretive, mysterious, pushy, controlling church on the other. Those diverse perceptions alone would suggest that perhaps it might be time to approach our image problem from a different angle.

Fortunately, a paradigm shift is already underway in the Church as indicated by the instruction we have received in recent General Conferences.

- Elder Dallin H. Oaks' address in October 2001 warned us against manipulation in missionary work, real or perceived, and suggested that talk of "missionary tools" may leave the impression that we want to manipulate people.

- Elder M. Russell Ballard told members in October 2006 that guilt has no place in teaching the gospel or motivating members.

- Elder Ballard's October 2007 address broadened the definition of success in spreading the gospel. The goal is no longer baptisms alone, but includes helping our friends gain a basic understanding of the Church, something every member has the ability to do.

- Elder Jeffrey R. Holland's address in the same session demonstrated ways to point out flaws in the sectarian creeds and how to engage those teaching false doctrines, a not-insignificant shift in Church diplomacy. His talk in the April 2008 Conference explained in a similar way the faulty reasoning employed by those who argue against latter-day revelation.

Using the above instructions as guidelines, let's change our thinking – let's turn away from the fears associated with past methods, eliminate feelings of pressure and guilt, learn to understand how our friends view the world, and redefine what it means to successfully communicate who we are and what we believe.

Channel Your Fears

We can improve our image more comfortably than we can do regular missionary work, but a few trepidations may linger. To minimize and learn to work around them, here are three approaches that may help.

First, we must understand that **a fear exists only if it threatens something we value**. Consider the following:

We value . . .	So we fear . . .
A comfortable status quo	Change
Our self-image	Anything that will embarrass us, result in ridicule
Intelligence	Appearing inadequate; saying the wrong thing
Reasonableness	Looking irrational, being viewed as zealots
Friendships	Losing a friend
Respect	Disrespect to ourselves or our investigator friends
Equality	Being treated as subordinate
Being ourselves	Undertaking uncomfortable roles
Our space	The pressuring or badgering of ourselves or our friends
Our religion	Anything that demeans it

The key is to **focus on our values more than on our fears**. If we focus on our fears, we exaggerate the anticipation that something negative will happen. By focusing on our values, including the ones we think may be threatened, we see the bigger picture and are less likely to exaggerate our fears. Focusing on a value connected to a fear reduces the fear.

For example, if we ask ourselves, "How can I talk about the ultimate thing I value – the gospel of Jesus Christ – in a way that does not threaten a friendship?" the chances are good that we will discover an acceptable balance between two good values. But if we ask ourselves, "How can I spread gospel information without looking weird?" fear wins and guilt is the result. We feel guilty that we have given in to our fears (looking weird), and we feel guilty that we have not been true to a value (spreading the gospel).

Fears and guilt occur together. Values and guilt generally do not. We must focus on our values.

The second approach to channeling fears is to realize that **our friends also have fears** about religious discussions. There are many who are curious about the Church but may be afraid to initiate a conversation because they fear . . .

- Confrontation
- Pressure
- Entrapment
- Arguments
- Not having adequate responses to questions we may ask
- Undermined beliefs
- Hearing more than they expect or want to hear
- A strained friendship

Our friends may sense that we are more knowledgeable about religious topics than they, so it is up to us to signal that we will not consider their questions an invitation to inundate them with everything we know. As we improve our abilities to engage in casual conversations about religion and employ the ideas in these chapters, our fears and the fears of our friends will fade into the background.

At the end of a focus group I conducted in Southern California testing a Church film, a young lady waited until the other participants had left and asked me if I was a Mormon. She then said she had Mormon neighbors that she was impressed with and wanted to ask them questions about their religion, but was embarrassed to do so. In other words, she was hesitant to initiate a conversation because she had the same fears we often have. If her neighbors had made even the most casual of references to the Church, it would have provided the opening she sought. As it was, I suggested that she now had a perfect reason to bring up the Church because she could tell her LDS neighbors that she had just participated in a focus group that tested a film about Joseph Smith. She said, "That's what I've been thinking." (If you ever read this book, Ms. B, let me know what happened.)

> Our own fears diminish when we worry less about how we feel and more about how others feel.

The results of two questions on the national survey provide a third way to place fears in proper perspective. Interviewers asked those who claim a denomination to compare what their own denomination teaches with what they personally believe, and then asked what percentage of their own belief system overlaps with their denomination's teachings – that is, how often both are in agreement.

Overlap of Personal and Denomination Beliefs

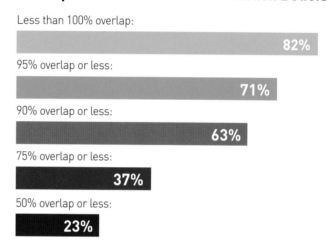

Less than 100% overlap:
82%

95% overlap or less:
71%

90% overlap or less:
63%

75% overlap or less:
37%

50% overlap or less:
23%

The average overlapping agreement is 75%, and the median score (where half scored above and half scored below) is 85%. Thus, when we talk to friends whom we feel may be firmly grounded in their own faiths, we should remember that the chances are good that many are more open to hearing other points of view than we may think.

Those who had less than a 100% belief overlap with their own denomination were asked on what doctrine they find themselves differing the most.

- Abortion   11
- Marriage / divorce   7
- Political positions   7
- Homosexuality   6
- Godhead   6
- Commandments   6
- Doctrines in general   6
- Hypocrisy / attitudes   6
- Practices   5
- Scriptures   5
- Afterlife   5
- Role of women   4
- Organization in general   4
- Birth control   3
- Other social issues   3

When people disagree with their churches, it more often has to do with current social behaviors than traditional theological doctrines. Many members might have an easier time discussing the latter, but knowing people's concerns about social issues may provide a useful way for us to open a conversation.

Also keep in mind that 38% of all Americans are no longer affiliated with the same religion they grew up in, according to my survey. Similarly, a recent study by the Pew Forum on Religion and Public Life reported that 44% have changed religions since their childhood.[21] Both studies indicate substantial fluidity, even volatility, in the American public on the topic of church membership. Although a great deal of the changing happened among Protestant denominations sharing similar viewpoints, Protestantism with its once robust majorities in America continues to lose ground and now stands at 51%, according to the Pew study. **Many people are looking for something better.**

Eliminate Pressure and Guilt

New thinking requires a new view of numbers. Properly used, numbers are good management tools, but they can also be an unrelenting taskmaster and source of guilt because no matter what numbers we achieve, there is always one higher. **The first step to eliminate pressure and guilt is to put numbers in their proper perspective**.

We do not put a number on love, faith, testimony, the sweetness of a newborn, the joy of a returning wayward child, the recovery of good health, or the reassurance of the resurrection at the funeral of a loved one. We count the things that can be counted, but the truly important things in life often cannot be counted. And I speak as a statistician.

So when it comes to improving the Church's image, we can free ourselves from numbers. We can minimize pressure. We need not count the number of times we follow any of the suggestions in this book. We should encourage fellow members to join us in taking steps to change our image, but we should not micromanage the process. Let's just do it and not worry about counting anything.

> *The older I grow the less concerned I become with quotas and statistics and percentages, and the more I become concerned with the kind of experience that the soul of man has in the Lord's church.*[22]
>
> - President Gordon B. Hinckley

> *Not everything that counts can be counted, and not everything that can be counted counts.*
>
> - Albert Einstein

Guilt often results when we feel we have not done enough to spread the gospel. Such counter-productive guilt drains our enthusiasm and must be ignored. We can do only so much, and we are only responsible for reasonable efforts, not the end results. People have their agency, and no amount of righteousness on our part can displace it. To feel that we have failed because a friend or acquaintance decides not to investigate the Church, even after we have improved our image in his mind, flies against gospel principles. As Elder M. Russell Ballard put it:

> Eliminate guilt. I hope it goes without saying that guilt is not a proper motivational technique for leaders and teachers of the gospel of Jesus Christ. We must always motivate through love and sincere appreciation, not by creating guilt.[23]

Sometimes pressure and guilt arise from our own misperceptions. For many years, the charge to "bear your testimony" produced a picture in my mind of taking a deep breath, clearing my throat, telling my listener that "I want to bear my testimony," and then saying something formal and profound about what I believe. That was the form I felt I was expected to follow. And I felt the pressure to perform.

Then one day I wondered how I would feel if someone of another faith said to me, "I want to witness to you ...". Would I feel comfortable and ready to listen, or would my defenses go up? The answer was obvious. When we identify a statement of belief as a testimony, the listener may feel he's in court and we're figuratively putting our hands on the Bible. There's a time to say, "I want to bear my testimony" such as during a formal teaching situation or on the first Sunday of each month, but it's a counterproductive phrase to use in day-to-day conversations.

In recent years I have come to know that bearing testimony can take many forms, and I dispel my self-imposed pressure by substituting phrases that work better in natural conversations:

Here's what I believe . . .

I feel that . . .

My point of view may be a little different, but my take on it is . . .

My position on that issue is . . .

All I can tell you is what I believe.

The best testimonies are often borne when the word testimony isn't mentioned.

Think Empathetically

I once asked an investigator to share with me his understanding of the Nicaean Council of 325 A.D. and the creeds that ensued from that conclave. He spoke in approving terms. The Council, in his mind, was the culmination of a long struggle to codify Christianity and represented a turning point that would spread Christ's gospel to the entire earth.

I then asked him his views of the early Christian church. He claimed that Christ did not form a church, but that that task had fallen to the apostles and post-apostolic leaders. In his view, Christ provided the teachings – the Beatitudes, the Golden Rule, and the parables – and His followers molded the movement into an organization.

Our perceptions of Christian history passed as two rowboats in the fog (ships in the night being too elegant a metaphor). He felt that early Christianity proceeded on an upward path, whereas we hold that original Christianity followed a downward path as the original organization, teachings, and ordinances deteriorated, and the authority to act in Christ's name was taken from the earth. New Testament evidence that survived the scissors of scribes plainly indicates that Christ Himself gave the world a perfect organization during his ministry.[24] But my friend and much of Christianity look at the Nicaean Councils as the verification from heaven (such as the 318-2 vote affirming the alleged inseparable physical nature of the Trinity after Emperor Constantine made his preference known) that the Christian church was finally organized and doctrine codified, and that they could sally forth into the world to bring Christ's good news to every nation, kindred, tongue, and people. In their view, Christianity was solidified during the 300 years following Christ's crucifixion, and its fortunes continued upward from there.

Considering these disagreements, we cannot assume that people will easily accept our belief that Christ Himself organized the Church, let alone that there was a subsequent apostasy of the breadth and scope we claim. We must learn to think empathetically – to see the world of religion through the eyes of others – so we will sense how to best present our claims to those who may not grant the premise upon which we explain the story of the apostasy and restoration. As I will detail later, it is not necessary for them to agree with our position before we can change their image of the Church, but **it is useful for us to understand their perspective so we can better explain our own**.

Redefine Success

A budding author calls a publishing house and asks, "How many words in the average novel?" "About 75,000." "Oh, good; I'm through."

Maybe, like the novice author, we need to redefine our goals.

As we have tried to persuade those of other faiths of the correctness of our claims, we have traditionally focused on baptisms as the measure of success. If our efforts led to a baptism, we were successful; if not, then we were supposedly something less than that. If that has been our take on the gospel-sharing process, then we must shift focus and allow ourselves to feel good about whatever contributions we are making to spread information and improve our image. There are many success points along the path of education and understanding:

- Success is living an exemplary Christian life. You may be the only Book of Mormon someone will ever read.

- Success is mingling with new people in the community.

- Success is having a conversation. Spreading information is spreading the gospel.

- Success is informing someone what we claim to be – the re-established original Church.

- Success is correcting a distortion about us. Such corrections open minds, break down rigid thought patterns, and cause people to wonder what additional perceptions about us may not be true.

- Success is showing someone the inside of a church building – that there is nothing weird about LDS meetinghouses.

- Success is giving a friend a gospel principle or fact to think about, whether expressed in religious or secular terms.

- Success is answering questions about the Church by email.

- Success is reinforcing truths a person has already discovered, such as belief in a Godhead of three separate Personages or in continuous revelation, even though his or her church may teach otherwise.

We must identify and apply creative ways to provide information and explanations that **help our friends understand what the Church is about**. If someone has a better grasp of our beliefs and doctrines today than he had yesterday, that is success because understanding is central to changing our image.

> *It is only by doing things others have not that one can advance.*
>
> - General George Patton

Think Simple

 **Simplicity is the ultimate sophistication.**

- Leonardo da Vinci

A man walks into a drugstore and asks,
"Do you have any acetylsalicylic acid tablets?"
The pharmacist says, "You mean aspirin?"
"Oh yes," replies the man, "I keep forgetting
that word."

Simple Speech: Cut the Jargon

The way we members speak often contributes to the world's view of us as a strange people. We have been known to say such things as, "The gospel has been restored and the keys of the priesthood are again on the earth." That statement is clear to us, but Mormon-speak can be all but incomprehensible to others.

> When Moroni, John the Baptist, Peter, James, and John, et al, appeared to the Prophet Joseph Smith, they did not address him in their native tongues. They addressed him in English, the language he understood.

In focus groups with those of other faiths, I have asked what they understand by the word *gospel*. Most think of Matthew, Mark, Luke, and John. Others say it means "the good news" of Christ's mission. Only a few know its true sense as the whole of Christianity – doctrines, ordinances, authority, and organization.

When I asked for their understanding of the word *restored*, they said it's what you do to Grandma's old dining room table or the '66 Mustang Grandpa has been storing in the garage.

Their answers did not suggest in the slightest that the object in point had been lost and then was returned; rather, they assumed the object had always been around but had lost luster and required repainting or refinishing. Not understanding how we use the word restored – as something that is re-established – makes it difficult for people to grasp that we are referring to a universal apostasy, that the true Church was taken from the earth, and that it has now been brought back.

I wonder how many people upon hearing our claim that the gospel has been restored walk away musing, "St. Matthew has a new coat of paint?"

Where we use the word *gospel*, others would use the word *Christianity*. Where we use the word *restored*, others would use the word *re-established*. I love the word *restoration* and its related forms for the great cause it signifies, but others may not readily understand it. As we open conversations with those of other faiths, **using the word *re-established* best conveys our meaning** and creates curiosity. We can later explain our particular use of the word *restored*.

So, instead of saying "The gospel has been restored," consider expressing the same idea in three sentences that anyone, regardless of religious background, can grasp:

- **Christ organized a church.**
- **Men changed it.**
- **It has been brought back.**

Or condense it to one simple claim:

We claim to be the re-established original Christian church.

> We do not communicate by saying something we understand, but by saying something our listener understands.

My wife Jan once asked rhetorically, "Why do we start with the third paragraph?" In other words, we often talk about the restoration before we have established whether the listener understands that Christ organized a Church (the first paragraph) and that there was a universal falling away from it (the second paragraph).

When the first paragraph (Christ organized a Church) was tested by itself, 48% said they believe Christ organized a church when He was on the earth. When given a choice between two explanations of how the original Christian church began, only 33% of non-LDS Christians said that Christ organized a church during His ministry, while 64% said that it was organized by His followers after His crucifixion.

Groups

Highest believing Christ organized the Church:

18-34, minorities, singles, widowed, Bible readers, Catholics, and women more than men

Groups

Highest believing Christ's followers organized the Church:

College and post-grads, liberals, Midwest, more than $50,000 annual income

The second paragraph, dealing with apostasy, was tested from three angles. While people rarely use the word apostasy in daily conversation . . .

- 74% of all Americans believe that men changed the original church.

- 44% of all Americans feel something is missing in religion today, including 22% who think their own religion has something missing; 51% are generally satisfied.

- 36% of all Christians, when asked to view Christianity today, feel that things are the way Jesus Christ intended, while 57% feel something went wrong along the way.

While most people may not quickly agree with our claim that Christ Himself organized His church during His ministry, they are more likely to believe that men changed the original church and/or that something went wrong along the way to make today's Christianity what it is. That is not a bad platform from which to state our claim that the original Church has been brought back.

In fact, when the third sentence (paragraph) of our restoration sequence was tested, people judged it thus . . .

Maybe Mormons are right

17%

Mormons are probably wrong

36%

Mormons are definitely wrong

29%

No opinion

18%

Obviously, before we can effectively provide facts and explanations that will improve our image, we must understand from what perspective people are likely to assess our claims. We must not overestimate people's knowledge of Christian history or assume that the next friend we talk to will become interested for the same reasons as the last one. Nor should we underestimate the possibility that a friend may hold beliefs closer to our own than we may think.

Groups

Highest feeling something went wrong:

Liberals, moderates, Independents, 55+, Midwest, college grads

We should not expect those of other faiths to understand our usage of gospel and restoration any more than we may understand their usage of the rapture or the great commission. Consider these other commonly used LDS terms that may be misunderstood:

Dispensation. We mean an era of time. Catholics understand it as special permission.

Priesthood. We know it to have two interrelated meanings: the power to act in God's name and those who hold that power. Many people in other faiths think only in terms of the human definition, such as pastors in priestly vestments.

Keys of the priesthood. We mean the power to direct the priesthood. Many others take the literal view of keys as the metal things priests use to lock and unlock church buildings.

Sacrament. Generally, as in sacrament meeting, we mean the sacrament of the Lord's Supper given to us in remembrance of His sacrifice. In Catholicism there are seven sacraments – baptism, confirmation, Eucharist, reconciliation (or penance), anointing of the sick, marriage, and holy orders.[25] So when we say, "Come visit sacrament meeting with me," a Catholic may wonder if he's going to view a baptism, a wedding, or last rites. It's always safe to use the phrase "worship services."

Saints. We know that a saint in New Testament usage was simply a member of the Church. Catholics, on the other hand, define saints as "those who have lived a holy life, who now share in the Beatific Vision (i.e., face-to-face experience of the presence of God), and who may be publicly venerated by the faithful." [26]

Atonement. The central doctrine of doctrines of the Church. We cannot fully understand its significance, grandeur, and power, but we know it consists of so much more than the resurrection and the hope of life after death, which is about as far as most religions go in trying to define it. What we know about the Atonement is largely due to the Book of Mormon and latter-day revelation. For the rest of the Christian world, the word atonement appears only once in the New Testament. Their understanding of what we mean will be limited, though the faith in Christ of some may even exceed ours.

And the list could go on – wards, stake centers, high council, Relief Society, pre-mortal existence, war in heaven, temple, endowment, gentile, Zion, tithing, mortality, apostasy, and so forth. It would take a small dictionary to house all of our terms.

It seems almost too obvious to note that we must judge how words familiar to us may strike someone from another religious upbringing. If a substitute word works, use it; otherwise, be sure to **define our meaning** before using our term.

> Learn to **use their words to express our concepts.** We can teach them our vocabulary later.

Reading the scriptures, I marvel at the Lord's ability to say so much in so few words. We, on the other hand, seem to measure success in words per minute.

> It's better to speak five words that teach, as Paul told the Corinthians, than 10,000 in an unknown tongue that may dazzle but not edify. [27]

During the Newport Beach temple open house, tour hosts were trained to follow a set of talking points. Some, however, were so enthusiastic to have a captive audience willing to learn something about our religion that, left to their own devices, they would not only have covered the talking points, but given all the missionary lessons plus the temple preparation seminar to boot. I'm convinced that those who gained the most from the tours were those who heard the fewest and simplest words.

In his October 2007 General Conference address, Elder Ballard said:

> Brothers and sisters, in today's busy world, I have found that most people will not read or focus on more than just a few important facts at one time. Whatever you choose to use to inform your friends and acquaintances about the Church, write it down, check it for accuracy, and keep it simple and short.[28]

Remember Professor Prothero's statement that America is "one of the most religious countries on earth [but] is also a nation of religious illiterates."[29] So don't use Sunday school language and don't pile it on. Boil it down; condense it. Find the clear phrase that will stimulate thought. Get the basics across and then wait. Either the person or a prompting will let you know when it's time to share the next piece of information.

People don't remember treatises; they remember short phrases and succinct concepts.

Simple Behavior: The Golden Rule

All efforts to improve our image begin with how we treat others. Are people objects to be manipulated or equals to be guided? Do we insist on control or give them latitude? Do we challenge or invite? Are we pushy or patient? Do we care more about our numbers or their welfare?

Is there a better time to demonstrate the Golden Rule than when someone is curious about the restored Church?

As noted earlier, in the October 2001 General Conference, Elder Dallin H. Oaks said:

> I hope no person we approach with an invitation to hear the message of the restored gospel feels that we are acting out of any reason other than a genuine love for them and an unselfish desire to share something we know to be precious. The need to act out of love also warns us against manipulation, real or perceived. People who do not share our belief can be repelled when they hear us refer to something as a 'missionary tool.' A 'tool' is something used to manipulate an inanimate object. If we talk about something as a 'missionary tool,' we can convey the impression that we want to manipulate someone. That impression is entirely contrary to the unselfish, sharing spirit of our missionary service.[30]

How we treat people determines not only who becomes truly converted and is still with us years later, but also how successful we will be in permanently improving our image. The assertive approach, so often found in circles of commerce, tends to work on the manipulable, while the Golden Rule approach appeals to the more secure and independent. Whether we seek only to improve the image of Mormonism, or whether we are fortunate enough to help friends seriously investigate the Church, note the differences between the two approaches.

> As in Aesop's fable of the sun and the wind arguing who can cause a man to remove his coat, the gentler approach is more effective than force and manipulation.

Two Human Relations Approaches		
	The Assertive Approach	**The Golden Rule Approach**
Technique	Maneuver and push	Befriend and mentor
Relationship	Dominant-subordinate	Equal-equal
Conversation	Challenge - Will you commit to ...?	Invite - What would you think about ...?
The person	Target to be maneuvered – a passive listener	Friend to be helped – an active student
Process	Teach until the person is willing to accept the gospel and be baptized	Guide self-learning until the person becomes converted and is prepared to live the gospel
Baptism	Result of pressure – agrees to be baptized	Natural result of active investigation and guided learning – asks to be baptized
Conversion	Outside in	Inside out
Timeline	Short	Open

President Gordon B. Hinckley specified the Golden Rule approach to those of other faiths when he said:

> As a church, we are not without critics, some of whom are mean and vicious. We have always had them, and I suppose we will have them all through the future. But we shall go forward, returning good for evil, being helpful and kind and generous. Let us be good people. Let us be friendly people. Let us be neighborly people. Let us be what members of The Church of Jesus Christ of Latter-day Saints ought to be.[31]

When a segment of my national sample was asked what advice they would give Mormons regarding the antagonism some Americans hold toward them, the top three answers were: be more open, ignore it, and be less pushy. In other words, follow the counsel of President Hinckley and extend the Golden Rule even to those who may not reciprocate.

Improving our image is easy when we, in the spirit of the Golden Rule, simply **tell people who we are and what we offer**.

> The most frequent word at the beginning of LDS hymns is the word "Come." This welcoming and invitational expression is the lead word of 22 hymn titles.

A Simple Model: Attention Levels

All of us would like to so improve our image in the minds of our friends that they would enthusiastically investigate the Church and be converted. This natural wish will remain with us as long as we are under the commandment to carry Christ's gospel to the four quarters of the earth. Yet to achieve our immediate image-building goal, the traditional find-teach-baptize model of regular missionary work falls short.

The six-stage model shown on the following page is an easier way to think about image building because it divides the education process into smaller steps and focuses on how people think about Mormons – their levels of attention – instead of focusing on baptism. As with all models of the Church journey, it designates conversion as the ideal end state. We know that we will not reach the sixth stage very often, but if we follow this model, and **understand how people think** in the first four stages, and especially the first three stages in which misperceptions flourish, we will become more adept at providing information at the appropriate time. We will, therefore, be less likely to rush the curious and the merely interested to baptism, thinking it synonymous with conversion, and be more likely to effectively change perceptions toward the Church among more people.

Of course, if friends reach the fourth stage and decide to take the next step and seriously investigate the Church, that would be wonderful, but if they do not, we still will have advanced the Church's image because **every misperception we correct means one less incorrect story on the grapevine**. The person with the corrected image of us may never join the Church, but will perhaps say something about us that will cause a third person to view us from a new perspective and become interested in what we offer. Here are the six steps and the thoughts that determine each:

Conversion

"I will help build the kingdom."

Investigation

"I have to know if this is true.
I will study and pray."

Interest

"This could be serious.
I will listen."

Curiosity

"I wonder what Mormons
believe about ..."

Awakening

"Why am I hearing so much
about Mormons lately?"

Awareness

"Mormons exist."

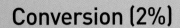

Conversion (2%)

"I will help build the kingdom."
LDS

Investigation (5%)

"I have to know if this is true. I will study and pray."
25-34, high LDS knowledge, minorities, no religion

Interest (9%)

"This could be serious. I will listen."
Widowed, minorities, non-Christians, 35-44, seniors, Protestants

Non-LDS participants in the national study were asked to indicate their relationship to Mormons by placing themselves in one of the first five stages:

All I know is that they exist	40%
I have noticed more stories about them lately	25%
I am a little curious about their religion and who they are	11%
I am interested in knowing what they believe	9%
I could see myself seriously investigating their religion	5%

Then the demographic groups were checked to see which ones were the highest in each of the stages:

Curiosity (11%)

"I wonder what Mormons believe about ..."
Divorced, Baptists, moderates, South

Awakening (25%)

"Why am I hearing so much about Mormons?"
College and post-grads, non-Christians, above $50K, married, 35-54

Awareness (40%)

"Mormons exist."
Less than HS, Baptists, singles, 25-34, below $50K

97

The model on the previous page leads to the question, "Where should we put our emphasis?" The missionaries in our midst will want to know how to find the 5% who are the potential serious investigators; our natural teachers will want to find the interested and the curious for the thrill of igniting the learning process; and the diplomats among us will want to reach out to the unaware and barely aware. For reasons we will subsequently explore, my conclusion is that we should not directly try to find people in any particular group. We will find them indirectly if we begin by treating everyone the same. Here's why.

If we seek only the potential investigator and assertively work to extract a referral for the missionaries, we will fail the vast majority of the time. There may be those in our ranks who are willing to offend 19 to get to the one, but we will pay, and unfortunately are already paying, a price by so doing. People who are pushed to talk to the missionaries before they, on their own, recognize a need to do so will be that much more vulnerable to the charges of our critics who point to our pushiness as an early warning indicator of force to come. We will continue to suffer a poor image.

But if we seek only to present a few facts in natural and friendly conversations and let things unfold how they will . . .

. . . the latent investigator will feel comfortable admitting to a serious interest;

. . . the appetite for learning among the curious and interested will be sharpened; and

. . . the two-thirds who know little to nothing about us – the group that can have the greatest impact on our overall image – will begin thinking . . . and changing.

We must break the false assumption that we are successful only if we deliver someone into a formal teaching setting. The majority of Americans need basic information about us. They do not need a fraternity swarm. If we will **relax and be content to contribute a few pertinent facts** as conversations warrant, we will foster the understanding of us that is so lacking, and improve our image in the process.

Understanding must always precede interest and investigation.

A self-referral growing out of friendly and natural conversations is more fruitful than a dozen extracted referrals.

Prepare the Stage

Chance favors only the prepared mind.

- Louis Pasteur

Joseph Smith was told by the angel Moroni that his "name would be had for good and evil" throughout the world.[32]   As this prophecy continues to be fulfilled, it is little wonder that impressions of us as a people are likewise both positive and negative, some people holding both images simultaneously.

On the whole, more people hold a negative impression of us than a positive one, but much of this could be reversed if people only had accurate facts. Though the Church regularly disseminates information about us through the mass media, our friends and acquaintances will give the same facts more credence, and remember them longer, if they hear them from us, the individual members, in normal conversations.

Before we can be successful in those conversations, however, we must set the stage by preparing our facts, expanding our circle of acquaintances, observing more carefully what's going on in our local communities, and increasing the buzz about us.

Prepare Facts

In the October 2007 General Conference, Elder M. Russell Ballard addressed the need to better inform our friends and acquaintances who we are and to help them "gain a basic understanding of the Church."[33] He further stressed that there is "a great need for clear, simple statements that present those who are curious with the basics about the Church as it is today"[34] and asked us to choose a few facts from four categories of information that we could present simply and succinctly:

Facts – our name, how we began, our headquarters, our prophet, number of members, our rate of growth, finances, unpaid clergy, both men women in positions of leadership, and our representation in government and the professions

Faith – the soul, God is our Father, Christ is the Son of God and our personal Savior, His atoning sacrifice, our core beliefs, the original church is restored along with the authority to act in God's name, apostles and prophets, the Bible, and the Book of Mormon as another testament of Jesus Christ

Family – our theology and lifestyles are family-centered, deep commitment to marriage, clarification of 19th-century polygamy, Sunday services, family home evenings, auxiliary programs, family history, and the most sacred ordinances of the temple relate to our families

Fruits – health code, longevity, low divorce rates, high educational level, volunteerism, missionary service, self-reliance, work ethic, and our humanitarian efforts throughout the world to alleviate suffering

He asked us to polish our choices into simple declarative sentences, keeping them simple and short. We do not have to prove, debate, persuade, or argue. We do not have to be eloquent, charismatic, brilliant, or charming. We should simply be ready to put an idea or two on the table – touch and go – to **give people facts to think about**.

> We must become for gospel truths what Johnny Appleseed was for apples.

103

Expand Your Circle

On a family vacation, my daughter Kristen decided that a full day of skiing had not been enough activity, so after the ski lifts closed, she and her sister Stephanie hauled a saucer sled to the top of a hill and pushed off. To a detached scientific observer, it might have appeared an experiment in whether the mass and velocity of two teenagers could move a tree. Answer: not even a millimeter.

My good neurosurgeon friend Lynn Gaufin met Kristen's life-flight at three in the morning and guided her recovery from a basal skull fracture that cracked her head like an egg shell and scrambled her arrays, so to speak. As she recuperated, she had a difficult time concentrating, but sitting at the piano and working through her music had a marvelous effect. Music helped her organize her thoughts and concentrate. It helped her regain her skills and self-confidence and she later graduated from BYU with a music degree in organ performance. (She is now composing and writing a book of Halloween carols.)

Because of this experience, my wife Jan joined a local group of women known as The Committees of the Philharmonic Society of Orange County, a volunteer organization dedicated to presenting music programs and concerts to school children. She felt passionately that experiencing musical performances could help children not only appreciate the beauty of music, but help them organize and think. Her people skills and leadership ability were soon recognized; she worked her way up in the organization and was elected president.

Has she spread the gospel in her position? Not if it is defined as giving referrals to missionaries and assisting someone to the waters of baptism. But has she improved our image? Yes. There are now upwards of 1000 women in her countywide organization who know they are rubbing shoulders with a bona fide, active Latter-day Saint. She has answered questions as they have come up – such as clarifying fuzzy information in the 2007 PBS series about us – but does not open conversations with the intention of converting anyone. She loves the women she works with and is simply herself.

The moral of this little story: **Find a cause you believe in and join a civic, service, or cultural organization.** It need not take substantial amounts of time or detract from your Church callings. Jan did it while teaching early-morning seminary for seven years and then serving as Relief Society president for five. Even a couple of hours a week dedicated to a volunteer organization in our communities will bless the lives of others and will improve the probabilities that someone may in time ask, "What is the difference between your church and mine?"

We members generally experience the greatest demands on our time between the ages of 25 and 45 as we raise families, establish careers, and are called to increasingly responsible positions in the Church. Then, about the time we reach age 45 or so, children leave home, careers are stable, and the most time-consuming callings begin to fall on younger members. High priests may be the most underutilized members we have.

Wouldn't our years after the age of 45 be a good time to get more involved in our communities? Given the training and experience in whatever callings have come our way, we (even those of us in the faithful-old-fossils category) could contribute significantly to the quality of our communities and in the process meet many good people. If nothing else, why not organize a neighborhood crime-watch program or a phone-tree or email contacting system to assist neighbors in case of emergencies?

There are many opportunities to erase the images left by such members as the inactive young man known for his ability to hold his beer.

Observe Social Dynamics

As Yogi Berra put it, "You can see a lot just by observing."

Consider two examples from the scriptures:

When the apostle Paul visited Athens about A.D. 53, he did not knock on doors but took the measure of the community by walking around the city and observing. He noted two things: first, that Athenians had many statues to their deities and superstitiously had dedicated one "To the Unknown God" lest perchance they offend a god they didn't know, and second, that Athenians and visitors alike spent their time telling or listening to "some new thing." Putting these facts together, Paul identified his opening to inject gospel teachings into the Athenian discussion.[35]

On the other side of the world, Ammon and his brethren, desiring to bring the gospel of Christ to the Lamanites, boldly stepped across the borders into the Lamanite kingdom. Beyond that, they did not have a plan. Ammon was captured and taken before the king, who, in an inspired moment of softness, inquired about his intentions. Ammon's comment that he desired to live among the Lamanites for a time, perhaps until he died, so pleased King Lamoni that he even tried to persuade Ammon to take a daughter off his hands.

Ammon stayed on task. He carefully observed the social dynamics at the waters of Sebus where he had been assigned to join other servants tending the king's sheep. When a marauding band drove off the sheep and the servants bewailed their anticipated death at the hands of the angry king, Ammon rejoiced. Here, after only three days of waiting, was his opportunity. After applying perhaps the first arms control measure in history, and gathering the scattered sheep, Ammon found himself in the court of a king who was ready to listen.[36]

Note that in both cases gimmicks were eschewed. Neither Paul nor Ammon ran up to someone waiting at a chariot stop and breathlessly exclaimed that they had an important message. **They watched until they understood the dynamics** of what was happening in the local community. Then they received promptings on how to deliver their messages.

We gain traction the same way.

- Listen to what people are talking about. What are the interests of our friends and fellow workers? What's going on in the community? What events are going on? Listen for mentions of the Church.

- Read and watch a broad sample of news media, from TV to the Internet. Look for stories, quotes, statistics, poll results, and events that mention the Church or its members.

- Watch for distortions about the Church in general conversations, Internet blogs, and other media.

- Think of ways to correct those distortions when the opportunity arises. And when an idea for a conversational comment strikes, ask whether it is **a clear thought that feels good,** the definition of a prompting that I have found most workable.

Increase the Buzz

Another way we prepare the stage is to get our communities talking about us. It's called buzz – the informal, word-of-mouth transfer of information.

A young man in my previous company was zealous in his demonstrations against the Church. Every Saturday would find him marching back and forth in front of the Los Angeles temple with placards similar to those seen near the Conference Center the first weekends of April and October.

One Friday evening as we wrapped up work, I flippantly said, "See you tomorrow morning at the temple." After a long pause with not a flicker of understanding on his face, I asked him, "Which do you think is the bigger problem for Mormons – antagonism or apathy?" The wattage began to rise. I said, "You and your friends are doing us a favor. Keep it up."

> *You have enemies? Good. That means you've stood up for something, sometime in your life.*
>
> *- Winston Churchill*

This young man and his friends created buzz. As people drove down Santa Monica Boulevard and saw a sign that said "Jesus is not Satan's brother," many had to think, "I wonder what that's all about?" He eventually tired of this exercise, and I wondered if deep down he didn't agree with me – they were helping us.

We need buzz. The worst thing that can happen to us, as far as image building is concerned, is to be ignored – to have no opposition with which to contrast. I once told an audience preparing to host a temple open house that if protestors did not demonstrate against us, they should go down to the local Rent-a-Mob and hire some.

Many of us dislike initiating a religious comment. But if there's a buzz about us in the community, we don't have to. **Buzz will increase curiosity** and prompt those of other faiths to ask us questions without our having to initiate the conversation.

Including negative buzz? Yes, especially negative buzz. Some members shy away from religious discussions centered on negatives, hoping instead for opportunities in an ideal world with only positive comments in play. But true to the law of opposition, we make our greatest progress when there are negative comments we can challenge. Such buzz allows us to replace distortions with truths, and do it without appearing pushy.

> Apathy is a greater enemy than antagonism.
> Be thankful for negative publicity.

In 2007, the PBS Series *The Mormons*, a Mississippi minister sending out false-dichotomy CDs (*Jesus Christ vs. Joseph Smith*), Reverend Al Sharpton and his biased remarks, cheap shots at Mitt Romney, the ongoing HBO *Big Love* series, and Mormon-sniping movies such as *September Dawn* and *Georgia Rule*, all gave us opportunities to open conversations. **Pray for more such opportunities.**

In the 1850s, a German professor in Dresden came across a book that was causing a buzz, *Die Mormonen* (The Mormons) by Moritz Busch, and was so intrigued by the specious logic of the author's contentions that he determined to check out this new religion for himself. A letter to the Church found its way to an apostle in Liverpool, Elder Franklin D. Richards, who quietly sent Elder William Budge to Germany to be the professor's private instructor, religious freedom being unknown in Saxony at the time. Soon several investigators were ready for baptism. Elder Richards traveled from England to perform the ordinances and there enjoyed a marvelous manifestation of the gift of tongues – neither the professor nor Elder Richards knew the language of the other, but as they spoke in their own languages, they could understand each other perfectly. [37]

The professor emigrated to America, continued his teaching, and was eventually called by Brigham Young to form an academy that grew to become BYU. The convert's name: Karl G. Maeser.

Thank you, Mr. Busch. Thank you for the buzz.

The spotlight on prominent Mormons and events will continue to stir a national buzz, and the Church with its media messages will produce whatever buzz it can from Salt Lake. But we can't look to Church headquarters to stir up buzz in all communities all the time. **We need to increase our own local buzz**. Here are a few ideas that one stake president, Allen Haynie of the Escondido California South Stake, is implementing:

- Mormon Helping Hands projects
- News releases related to stake activities
- Op-ed columns
- Letters to the editor
- Radio talk-show appearances
- Youth service projects

- Presentations of our beliefs to high school classes
- Presentations to college classes
- Speeches to civic and service organizations
- City council resolutions
- Neighbor Helping Neighbor programs
- Family history fairs
- Emergency preparedness fairs
- Local blogs and threads

As it is now, people get information about us most frequently from the media rather than from members. My national survey asked people to think of the last thing they happened to hear, read, or otherwise find out about the Mormon religion, and to identify the source of that piece of information. Here are the top answers:

Media	30%
Friends, co-workers, relatives	14%
Members	10%
Missionaries	8%
Romney's political campaign	7%
Internet	6%
Books	6%
Literature, pamphlets	4%

On any given day, people may find information about us from a variety of sources. The media will still dominate, but notice how many say they heard something from a friend, a co-worker, or a relative. **The grapevine is alive and well, and we must feed it**.

We can also create significant buzz by talking directly about religious doctrines in community forums, media interviews, letters to the editor, or Internet blogs. Elder Jeffrey R. Holland blazed this path by addressing two faulty doctrines in his October 2007 and April 2008 conference talks – the Trinity creeds and the heavens-are-closed position on revelation.

Regarding the first of these, seven out of ten American Christians subscribe to the three-in-one concept of the Godhead as found in the Nicaean and related creeds, yet almost a fourth of our Christian neighbors already agree with our opposite teaching (the highest scores coming from those who do not pray, read the Bible, or attend religious services – rejection of this creed being somewhat correlated with rejection of all religious practices). Here are the key points from Elder Holland's October 2007 General Conference address:

> Our first and foremost article of faith . . . is "We believe in God, the Eternal Father, and in His Son, Jesus Christ, and in the Holy Ghost." We believe these three divine persons constituting a single Godhead are united in purpose, manner, testimony and mission. . . . I think it is accurate to say we believe They are one in every significant and eternal aspect imaginable except believing Them to be three persons combined in one substance, a Trinitarian notion never set forth in the scriptures because it is not true. . . .

> . . . the Nicaean Creed, with later reformulations such as the Athanasian creed . . . declared the Father, Son, and Holy Ghost to be abstract . . . and unknowable . . . separate persons, but they are a single being . . . three distinct persons, yet not three Gods but one . . . [and that the] three persons are incomprehensible, yet it is one God who is incomprehensible. We agree with our critics on at least that point – that such a formulation for divinity is truly incomprehensible. . . .

> . . . if one says Mormons are not Christians because we do not hold a fourth- or fifth-century view of the Godhead, then what of those first Christians, many of whom were eyewitnesses of the living Christ, who did not hold such a view either? . . .

> We declare it is self-evident from the scriptures that the Father, the Son, and the Holy Ghost are separate persons, three divine Beings, noting such unequivocal illustrations as the Savior's great Intercessory Prayer . . . His baptism at the hands of John, the experience on the Mount of Transfiguration, and the martyrdom of Stephen – to name just four. [38]

This address is full of statements that will cause buzz and stimulate people to think. If I had the opportunity to contribute only one sentence about this doctrine, it would be that three Gods in one is non-scriptural, illogical, and incomprehensible. And many people, on reflection, would find it hard to argue the opposite.

In the April 2008 General Conference, Elder Holland addressed his remarks about a second faulty doctrine to those who "have declared that there can be no more authorized scripture beyond the Bible."

> One of the arguments often used in any defense of a closed canon is the New Testament passage recorded in Revelation 22:18: "For I testify unto every man that heareth the words of . . . this book, If any man shall add unto these things, God shall add unto him the plagues that are written in this book." However, there is now overwhelming consensus among virtually all biblical scholars that this verse applies only to the book of Revelation, not the whole Bible. Those scholars of our day acknowledge a number of New Testament "books" that were almost certainly written after John's revelation on the Isle of Patmos was received. Included in this category are at least the books of Jude, the three Epistles of John, and probably the entire Gospel of John itself. Perhaps there are even more than these.

> But there is a simpler answer as to why that passage in the final book of the current New Testament cannot apply to the whole Bible. That is because the whole Bible as we know it – one collection of texts bound in a single volume – did not exist when that verse was written. For centuries after John produced his writing, the individual books of the New Testament were in circulation singly or perhaps in combinations with a few other texts but almost never as a complete collection. Of the entire corpus of 5,366 known Greek New Testament manuscripts, only 35 contain the whole New Testament as we now know it, and 34 of those were compiled after A.D. 1000.

> The fact of the matter is that virtually every prophet of the Old and New Testament has added scripture to that received by his predecessors.

> Continuing revelation does not demean or discredit existing revelation. The Old Testament does not lose its value in our eyes when we are introduced to the New Testament, and the New Testament is only enhanced when we read the Book of Mormon: Another Testament of Jesus Christ.

Were those early Christians who for decades had access only to the primitive Gospel of Mark ... offended to receive the more detailed accounts set forth later by Matthew and Luke, to say nothing of the unprecedented passages and revelatory emphasis offered later yet by John? ....

Since it is clear there were Christians long before there was a New Testament or even an accumulation of the sayings of Jesus, it cannot therefore be maintained that the Bible is what makes one a Christian.

So the scriptures are not the ultimate source of knowledge for Latter-day Saints. They are manifestations of the ultimate source ... the living God. [39]

There is a place in religion for pastels and nuances, but not when we are competing for the world's attention. If we are too timid to challenge false doctrine and distortions, we deserve to be the most misunderstood religion in the world.

The best buzz-causing statement in this address is the direct rebuttal to those who misunderstand Revelation 22:18 – that other books were written after Revelation, and that the Bible as we know it was not compiled as a book when that verse was written.

Fortunately for our efforts, 83% of all non-LDS Christians believe religious revelation is still possible today, while only 10% believe it stopped with the death of Christ's apostles, an indication that many ministers and pastors are out of step with their flocks.

Pointing out where we differ from other faiths not only creates buzz, but improves our image, regardless of whether our listeners agree or disagree with us, because **all clarifications, to one degree or another, reduce suspicions**. When people know where we stand, our opponents cannot take advantage of an atmosphere of uncertainty to transmit their half-truths and rumors.

Have Natural Conversations

Opinions cannot change facts,
but facts can change opinions.

The Lord told Joseph Smith in Liberty Jail:

For there are many yet on the earth among all sects, parties, and denominations, who are blinded by the subtle craftiness of men ... and who are only kept from the truth because they know not where to find it....[40]
[Emphasis added.]

Why do these many people from all walks of life, now as well as then, know not where to find the truth? Because, to put it bluntly, **we have not told them**. To be sure, we have beamed a variety of messages to the world – from the profound to the warm and fuzzy – but, for whatever reasons, only a small percentage know what we claim to be, and fewer still have any depth of knowledge. We have not counteracted the subtle craftiness of men by telling the world the most important and differentiating facts about us in **simple words they can understand**.

Isn't it about time ... for us to orient the world to our beliefs?

Start With a Parenthetical Mention

Few of us feel comfortable stating straight out, "I'm a Mormon," yet we want to signal that we are LDS in case the person with whom we are conversing has an interest. I have found a comfortable way to do this, and I call it the parenthetical mention, or the side comment.

The parenthetical mention is like the meat in a sandwich – it's the filling between two other comments. Here's the recipe:

> One primary comment
> One parenthetical mention
> One secondary comment

And here's an example of how it works in conversation:

> I had to go to Salt Lake last week on business, so I scheduled an extra day and took my daughter, who goes to BYU, skiing at Sundance. Great powder.

Note the simple plug-in formula:

Primary comment:	Business trip to Utah
Parenthetical mention:	Daughter at BYU
Secondary comment:	Went skiing on great snow

The person I'm conversing with now has several choices of where to take the conversation. He can ask me what business I'm in, who my client is in Utah, how often I go there, how I like powder skiing, what my daughter is studying, or make other comments about the state, business, recreation, or family. Or, he can pick up on the LDS connection: "Your daughter goes to BYU? Are you Mormon?"

The idea is to **present several conversational paths** and allow the person to choose which one he'd like to go down. You haven't brought an elephant into the room, so no one feels uncomfortable. If he picks up on the religious affiliation, let the conversation unfold as it will, but resist the temptation to say too much. If he does not pick up on it, his remembering that you're a Mormon may still be fruitful in a future conversation.

To make the parenthetical mention work, prepare two or three phrases and keep them in mind. Examine your life and identify the things that distinguish you as LDS. Polish them so that you're prepared to drop them in a parenthetical mention. Remember what Winston Churchill said about his impromptus.

Is there a parenthetical comment waiting to be crafted from these questions?

- Were you born in Utah?
- Have you ever lived in Utah?
- Did you serve a mission?
- Do you speak a foreign language because of that mission?
- Did you attend a Church-affiliated school?
- Did or do your children attend a Church school?
- Where were you married?
- Are you a convert?
- Who introduced you to the Church?
- What doctrine attracted you to investigate the Church?
- Was there a sociological attraction to the Church that you could mention?
- What calling do you have in the Church?
- What unique experiences have you had in the Church?

As an example, my oldest daughter Stephanie keeps her email address with a BYU Internet service provider so the suffix "@byu.net" signals her religious connection every time she sends an email. Similarly comfortable ways to indicate that we are LDS will be somewhere in our Church-related experiences, and the sooner we drop them into a conversation, the sooner we will find those like the focus group participant who was too embarrassed to initiate a religious discussion with her Mormon neighbors.

Understand the Power of a Comment

Telling a friend a few facts about us may seem inconsequential, but a simplified visual explains why planting even one or two facts in a person's mind can have a great impact.

Speaking metaphorically, when we are born, our mortal minds are clean landscapes. With every stimulus we experience, a dot settles on that mental terrain – call it a data point, a cognitive bit, or simply a piece of information. As we grow to understand relationships between dots, our brains create mental mailboxes, or mental files (I use them interchangeably), in which pieces of related information are stored. Soon there are billions of dots and mailboxes on our mental countryside, our sum total of trying to understand the world.

When a new bit of information lands on the scene, it's a wandering data point waiting for the mind to test possible fits and send it to the appropriate mental address. The mind, seeking harmony between and within its mental files, experiments with it. What is its nature? With what previously sorted information might it belong? Does it belong in this mental mailbox or in that one over there? Or does it require the creation of a new mailbox? The mind sooner or later decides where it best fits, and the data point is stored in that mental file. At any particular time there are many pieces of information floating around the mental landscape until they arrive at the most appropriate mailboxes.

This process of finding a fit for new information in an atmosphere of uncertainty is germane to how images of and interest in Mormonism are formed. Telling people one of our facts or claims introduces uncertainty into a more or less harmonious mental landscape, and people tend to either like or dislike such uncertainty. Of course, life does not cleanly divide us into two groups, but in general terms we either tolerate well or not so well the dissonance our experiences bring us. A psychology book might label the two groups *high dissonance tolerance* people and *low dissonance tolerance* people, but I think their orientation toward uncertainty is better captured for our purposes by calling them Explorers and Avoiders.

Explorers, more willing to tolerate uncertainties and more curious about life, will take a fresh piece of information about Mormonism and examine it in relation to all the other stick 'um notes found in that mental file. They will take the time to ponder it. Avoiders, on the other hand, will place the fact in the Mormonism mailbox, but will not be as interested in fitting the facts together. The mailbox door is closed, and the Avoider's mind thinks it has again achieved harmony, as this piece of information no longer floats around the mental landscape causing uncertainty and dissonance. Everything is in its place. ("A Bible, a Bible, we have got a Bible. . ." [41])

To obtain a rough feel for the distribution of these two groups in society, respondents in the February survey were asked to agree or disagree with one simple sentence: "I tend to enjoy the uncertainties of life." Not the most robust explication of this concept, but sufficient for our purposes as we found that 60% of Americans classify themselves as Explorers and 33% as Avoiders.

I tend to enjoy the uncertainties of life:

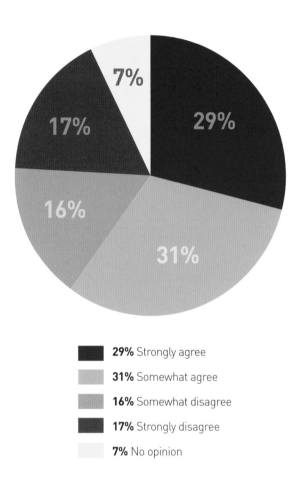

29%	Strongly agree
31%	Somewhat agree
16%	Somewhat disagree
17%	Strongly disagree
7%	No opinion

This means that the majority of Americans have a key trait of the Explorer personality. They are more likely to tolerate the dissonance and uncertainty that will come with our claim to be the original Church. Therefore, **our bold and simple message will fend for itself if we but place it on a listener's mental terrain**. The Explorers we seek, even those who may have previously rejected us, will be open-minded enough to think carefully about our claim if approached the right way.

State Our Claim

In late August of 1939 as the outbreak of World War II was imminent, several American missionaries serving in Germany were unaccounted for and had not checked in at the mission homes in either Holland or Denmark as instructed. Elder Norman Seibold, a missionary from Idaho, was sent from Copenhagen back into Germany to find and evacuate his fellow servants who were stranded without money and unable to get out. Guided solely by the Spirit, he would ride the train and wait for promptings. When such impressions came to him, he would get off and in the crowded, pre-war chaos of railroad stations whistle "Do What Is Right." Any missionaries in the crowd would recognize the hymn and were soon on a train heading to Denmark. Elder Seibold would then reboard the train and repeat the process on down the tracks until all missionaries had been safely evacuated.[42]

Stating our claim is like whistling the hymn the missionaries heard. The right people will respond to it. Elder Seibold did not use a trumpet nor whistle at 120 decibels. He only whistled loudly enough to communicate a bold message, and so it is as we present facts. The Lord's sheep shall hear His voice through us.

A major theory of this book is that if more people only knew what we claim to be, it would change our image, even if that knowledge never leads to one additional conversion.

Dr. Richard L. Bushman, noted LDS scholar and author, labels the coming era the "New Age of Conversation." He says that instead of proclaiming the gospel under our traditional definition, we will, without preaching or debating, "converse candidly in a straightforward way with curious outsiders and contribute to mutual understanding."[43] We will still be proclaiming the gospel as charged, but doing it in a different, less threatening way. It is the pattern, he points out, that President Gordon B. Hinckley used throughout his life, his interviews with the media being a form of conversation – state our claim, offer an explanation, reinforce the truths people already have, and invite them to consider more. The warning voice will still be there, but in mildness and meekness, as originally intended.[44]

There comes a time to simply drop comments into conversations and see what happens. I cannot provide you with a foolproof formula how to do it. I only know that if we are sensitive to conversations and social dynamics, we will find many opportunities to state our claim and do so comfortably. We will feel when we are being nudged by the Spirit to say something.

Not long ago, for example, I had just used a parenthetical mention to signal my religious affiliation to a medical technician when she replied, "Oh, I used to date a Mormon in high school." We talked about her experience, which was positive, and then I asked, "Did he ever tell you our main claim?" She said she had heard something about Joseph Smith and the Book of Mormon, but asked what I meant. I continued, "We make a claim that has three parts" and went on to state them. She said, "I didn't know that." Now she's part of the 14% who know our claim, and that's where I left it. It was simple and comfortable, even with two other people in the room.

We realize at least three benefits when we tell people what we claim to be.

The first benefit is that our claim **gives structure to people's perceptions of us and clears up confusion**. If we could see the average person's mental file labeled Mormonism, it would be an unorganized mish-mash of data points without structure. We would find random impressions from polygamy to Utah to a golden bible to temples to missionaries to Donny and Marie. People hear rumors, read inaccurate news stories, and listen to the far-fetched claims of our critics. They do not know which information is true. And even if they did, they still might not know how the pieces of Mormonism fit together.

The beauty of our simple claim to be the re-established original Church is that it will trigger a file-organizing process. When people understand what we claim to be, whether they believe that claim or not, they will finally have a nucleus data point around which to organize and better understand all the other items that have found their way into their Mormonism mailbox. Without this orienting claim, warped perceptions about us will continue to flourish in a fact-poor atmosphere and will hinder our efforts to change our image.

The second benefit from planting our claim in people's heads is that it **provides a defense** for those who are curious. If people do not know what we claim to be, why should they be interested in what we have to say? But if they do know our claim, they will feel their interest is justified because the claim gives them a logical defense against the criticisms of family and friends. They will not see themselves interested in a church (or a cult, as their friends may charge) held in disfavor by half of their fellow citizens, but will view themselves as reasonable, logical people who are interested in checking out a church that may actually be the original Church. **That possibility is all we need to plant**. Don't underestimate the spine-stiffening power our claim gives to the honest in heart.

The third benefit is that our claim **changes thought processes**. People can argue whether we are or are not the re-established original Church, *but they cannot argue the fact that we make that claim*. Simply by making that claim, we fluidize minds. This strong, bold claim not only forces a broad reframing of questions about us, but prompts fair and honest people to think, "Maybe I was wrong about Mormons not being Christians (or not believing the Bible, or whatever else). And if so, what else might I have wrong about them?"

It has been said that the media may not be too successful telling us what to think, but they are very successful telling us what to think about. The same is true of us. Our statements to friends may not convince them that our message is true, but may be very successful getting them to think about it.

> If we do not place information in people's mental mailboxes, the adversary will.

Our simple claim disturbs the mental status quo and gives the Holy Ghost something to testify to. The person who follows the logic chain leading from our bold claim and wonders whether he or she has been wrong about us is actually doing what the Lord requires before the Holy Ghost testifies: studying things out and keeping an open mind, of which this pondering is an example. If such people are the Lord's sheep, the claim sets in motion their journey to the truth.

An LDS girl, preparing for college, began working at a grocery store where a young Catholic man was earning his way through life. In time, religion came up among their group of workers and a returned missionary friend of the girl gave this young man the Joseph Smith pamphlet. After reading the tract, he confronted the girl, told her it was all a pack of lies, and that her church could not possibly be the true church. The girl replied in one simple sentence, "Well, it either is or it isn't."

This man later told me that her words had such a profound impact on him that he could not get that sentence out of his mind. It worked on him for weeks until he decided that he had to find out for himself whether "it is or it isn't." The wheels of conversion were put in motion.

About the same time, a few miles away, another young man overheard a Mormon girl at his high school tell her friends that she could never imagine herself getting married anywhere but in the temple. He thought, "What's so special about a building that she would say such a thing?" He, too, decided to find out. Again the wheels of conversion were put in motion by a simple statement.

These two girls did not know at the time the impact of their words. (And, no, they did not marry the young men in these stories.) Both men studied the gospel, became converted, and served missions. They now reside in the Orange California Stake – Dana Del Francia is on the high council and James Graham is a counselor in the stake presidency. All because of two simple statements.

Neither girl attempted to persuade, convince, or convert. Neither had the talents of a Cicero, a Demosthenes, or a Ronald Reagan. They did not marshal fancy arguments; they did not pile on words; they did not see themselves as formal missionaries. Simple statements put the wheels of conversion in motion ... and each one of us can do the same.

> *...by small and simple things are great things brought to pass.*[45]
>
> *- Alma the Younger*

> We do not have to reinvent the wheel.
> We only need to give it a push.

Use Humor

Humor is an underused weapon in our fight against ignorance, bigotry, and fear. President Gordon B. Hinckley said:

> We need to have a little humor in our lives. We better take seriously that which should be taken seriously, but at the same time we can bring in a touch of humor now and again. If the time ever comes when we can't smile at ourselves, it will be a sad time.[46]

If we occasionally **poke gentle fun at ourselves** as we convey our facts and claims, we smooth the conversation and disarm fears. One opening I use is "You've heard about Jewish mothers? Let me tell you about Mormon fathers." (I'll apologize to my dad when I get to the other side.) It breaks the ice and I tell some humorous story from my childhood that may trigger a question or two about the Church. If not, my listeners may still carry away an impression that they have nothing to fear from Mormons, no matter what our conversion rate or who holds public office.

> Slightly self-deprecating humor builds trust.

President Ronald Reagan was a master at disarming tense situations and countering attacks on supposed weaknesses in his character (that he was moribund, stupid, lazy, old) by addressing them head on with humor. Dumb like a fox, he knew exactly what he was doing:

I have left orders to be awakened at any time in case of national emergency, even if I'm in a cabinet meeting.

But there are advantages to being elected President. The day after I was elected, I had my high school grades classified as Top Secret.

It's true hard work never killed anybody. But I figure, why take the chance?

Thomas Jefferson once said, "We should never judge a president by his age, only by his works." And ever since he told me that, I stopped worrying.

President Hinckley was also known for his gentle humor and often directed it at himself. In his first address to a General Conference in 1958, he compared his new calling as a General Authority to an occasion on his mission when he was transferred to the European Mission office. He told the audience that his companion at the time said, "You must have helped an old lady across the street in the pre-existence. It isn't anything you've done here."[47]

And the time he kidded with a group of missionaries: "You may not be much to look at, but you're all the Lord's got."

There are many jokes and one-liners on the Internet about us, but the best use of humor is when we tell our own stories as members of the Church. Think of the topics open for gentle humor about us as a people: our food storage, riding bicycles on missions, meetings and more meetings, no drinking or smoking, stories about primary children, stories about teenagers in our youth programs, family home evenings, and the list goes on. We have a plethora (I've always wanted to use that word) of topics to plumb. The guideline is to comment or tell stories that are interesting and humorous, but which avoid insider humor, such as "knee fights" or "lame nights" word play.

How long would misperceptions of our potential use of political power stir fears if more of us would tell humorous stories about ourselves?

Mormons are pretty good at telling jokes on themselves, and I think it's a sign of our maturity when we can do that without diminishing our own convictions.

- Dr. Richard Bushman

Expand the Vision

 Nothing of importance happened today.

- Diary of King George III
   July 4, 1776

This and the following chapter suggest ideas for improving our image beyond identifying the few facts we prepare for the preliminary conversation discussed in Step Four. We do this by providing enough in-depth information so that our friends will correct distortions about us when we are not present to correct misunderstandings ourselves – in a phrase, by expanding their vision about what's really going on.

Know What's Missing

Before we can expand the vision people have of this work they call Mormonism, we have to **know what they want to know.**

I once helped teach an investigator who said he was Protestant. Seeking to build a bridge to his religious background as a way to introduce the Restoration, I put a few historical points about the Reformation on the table. Warming to the task, I referred to Martin Luther and explained how he, himself, admitted that he was not authorized to form a church and that he only wanted to return Catholicism to its original roots. I paused after what was to me, at least, a solid bridge-building feat and waited for his reaction. The young man said only, "Pardon me, but who is Martin Luther?"

As I quickly learned, we cannot truly communicate until we have invested the time to learn what our conversational partners understand and what they do not. And that means we must **get people talking about themselves**.

Evidence of a desire for straightforward information came in the national survey when respondents were asked what three questions they would want a Mormon acquaintance to answer about Mormonism. Here are the top areas of interest that at least 5% of the population would ask questions about:

Polygamy	Book of Mormon
Jesus Christ	Joseph Smith / Prophets
Beliefs	Marriage / Family
History	Lifestyle
Temples	Bible
Heaven / Afterlife	

Once they move beyond the stereotype of polygamy, people want to know the basics – **they want to know differences**. How they phrase their questions indicates two types of people: those who are unfamiliar with the basics of our religion and want to be better informed, and those who are cynical in that they assume we hold a particular belief and then ask argumentative, straw-man questions. They are either open-minded or closed-minded; few would ask a mix of information-seeking and hostile questions:

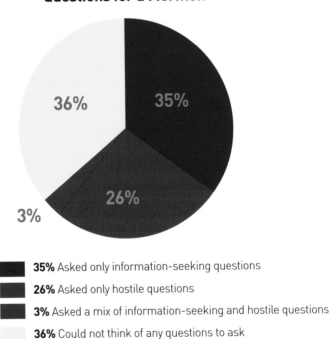

Questions for a Mormon

- **35%** Asked only information-seeking questions
- **26%** Asked only hostile questions
- **3%** Asked a mix of information-seeking and hostile questions
- **36%** Could not think of any questions to ask

Here are examples of the questions Americans would ask in their own words and the percentage falling into each group.

Examples of Questions People Would Ask of Mormons			
Topic	**Information-Seeking Questions**	**Hostile Questions**	**Total**
Polygamy	"Do they really believe in polygamy?" (9%)	"What's it like to have three wives?" (5%)	14%
Jesus Christ	"What are their beliefs about Jesus Christ?" (10%)	"How could you not believe Jesus is our Lord and Savior?" (2%)	12%
Beliefs	"I would ask what their religious beliefs are." (9%)	"How can you base such beliefs off so few facts behind it?" (3%)	12%
History	"What's the history of their church beliefs?" (4%)	"I would ask them if they know the factual history of their leaders." (5%)	9%
Temples	"I would want to know about the inside of the temple. . . the rituals that they complete in the temple." (4%)	"I want to know about the magic underwear." (5%)	9%
Afterlife	"What are their beliefs regarding the different levels of heaven?" (6%)	"Why can't they go to heaven if they have a baby from someone that isn't a Mormon?" (2%)	8%
Book of Mormon	"I would ask questions about the Book of Mormon." (4%)	"Why the archeological records don't support the Book of Mormon?" (4%)	8%
Joseph Smith / Prophets	"Is there some more information on Joseph Smith?" (4%)	"Why do they give Joseph Smith supremacy over Jesus Christ?" (4%)	7%
Marriage / Family	"I would like to know about their stand on marriage." (4%)	"Don't you think keeping your family size down is a good idea?" (3%)	7%

Examples of Questions People Would Ask of Mormons			
Topic	**Information-Seeking Questions**	**Hostile Questions**	**Total**
Lifestyle	"I would ask them about their way of life." (2%)	"Why can't a person experience life a little?" (4%)	6%
Bible	"Where do they stand on the word of God and the Bible?" (3%)	"Why don't they use the entire Bible?" (3%)	6%
Women	"How does their congregation treat women?" (2%)	"How could you believe that men are superior to women?" (1%)	3%
Missionaries / Converts	"I wonder whether they were a convert or born into it." (1%)	"Is it normal to have their missionaries track people down to get them to become members?" (2%)	3%
Christian	"How is it compared to other Christians?" (2%)	"Why do they claim to be a Christian religion when their big philosophy claims Christianity is not a true religion?" (0.5%)	2%
Financial, Tithing	"What about Mormons' financial system, and how does it work and why?" (2%)	"Why do you think you can get your heavenly rewards on earth in the form of monetary success?" (1%)	2%
Leaders	"Do they believe in whoever is their leader?" (0.5%)	"Why are they following people other than Jesus Christ?" (2%)	2%
Secrecy	"I would like to find out more about the mystical aspects of their church." (0.5%)	"Why do you have to be so secretive?" (2%)	2%
Political Issues	"What is the Mormon position on abortion and gay rights?" (1%)	"I don't understand how you could hate someone for being gay when they are born that way." (1%)	2%
Miscellaneous	(2%)	(3%)	5%
Don't Know / None			36%

And in the are-we-from-the-same-planet category:

"Why are the hats so important?"

"What is with the gold underwear?"

"I would ask why they use red dye and water as opposed to wine?"

"I would ask if they're allowed to date?"

"Why must they go to the beehives?"

Several things stand out from these findings:

- As indicated by the number and wide range of basic questions, we have assumed for too long that Americans know more about us than they actually do.

- This wide range of questions is not unexpected; remember that 65% of the people are in the "awareness" or "awakening" categories.

- Most questions asked of us will not be hostile. Most people simply want to know the facts.

- Our relationship to Jesus Christ is the single most substantive topic people will ask about. As we respond to such questions, it would be difficult for us to overemphasize our worship of Him, our belief in His divinity, our gratefulness for His Atonement, and our claim that He stands at the head of the Church. We must tell the world more of what we know about the Savior.

- It is interesting that only 2% had any questions related to God Himself, and only 1% about the Trinity. People already believe God is a personal God who has a plan for our lives, a point where we think we're different. They assume that there are few distinguishing differences between themselves and us on this topic or they would have asked more questions about it.

- If people are willing to ask one question, they're willing to ask several, because formulating one question helps them realize how much they don't know. Place one answer on their mental maps and there's a good chance that additional questions will line up in their mental queue.

- The above findings help us anticipate in a general way what people might find interesting. In actual conversations, however, we must listen carefully to determine what interests our listeners.

- While only 25% admit to curiosity, interest, or the possibility of a serious investigation, far more than that (64%) will ask questions if the circumstances are right.

The questions are there and we are more than willing to answer them. So why don't more people open up and ask them? **Might it be that we are not providing them a comfort zone free from pressure?** Or, to put it more starkly, freeing them from the fear of being led down a verbal cattle chute? We must earn their trust so we can provide facts and reassure them that asking a question or two will not lead them to a slippery slope they do not want to slide down.

It is a shame that, in this age of instant communication, so many people would still not know our position on polygamy and that it would lead the list of questions people would ask about us. We have tried for over a century to correct the misperceptions, but these facts remain:

- 85% are not sure whether we practice polygamy or not.

- Polygamy is the number one thing people say they like least about us.

- It is the subject of the first question they would ask a Mormon.

- It even came up in a right-brain association question.

Two points need to be made here. First, polygamy remains a barrier to the flow of information about us. Mistaken identity provides a convenient excuse for some who wish to avoid a serious investigation of our message. People avoid studying religions that carry stigmas.

Second, the confusion about who is and who is not a Mormon will not fade away by itself. The survey results demonstrate that the misperception is entrenched in America's collective psyche.

Therefore, we members must not be shy about correcting the record. Many Americans are looking for a definitive answer and want to believe that we are not polygamists, but we must present information differently from the way we have in the past. We must break the stereotype by giving them new, perhaps even humorous, angles to emphasize what the truth is. Thanks to my good friend Glen Greener, here are a few statements that I have found useful (and enlivening) in conversations:

- If you want to be quickly excommunicated from the Mormon Church, marry a second wife. All other sins take longer.

- If I were to start a new church, putting the word "Fundamentalist" in front of the word "Lutheran," for example, would not make me a Lutheran.

- There are over 150 breakaway groups from the LDS Church, some of which practice polygamy. We are not part of them and they are not part of us.

- People will eventually find out that we Mormons no longer practice polygamy. So, in the big scheme of things, I would prefer to be wrongly called a polygamist who doesn't polyg, than a monogamist who doesn't monog. *

In a more serious vein, I sometimes openly share my frustrations and tell my acquaintances that many people looking for a religion would check out our church if it weren't for the false association with polygamy: **All we ask is that people know the facts.** What they do with those facts is up to them.

*Statement attributed to Senator Boies Penrose in 1903.

Use Contrast

Shortly before he died, Lehi explained existence to his son Jacob in one of the most powerful chapters in the Book of Mormon.[48]   As pure philosophy, let alone religious doctrine, it ranks among the most stimulating intellectual treatises ever written. Lehi takes the simple revelation – that there must be an opposition in all things – and builds on it to produce deep insights.

He explains that without opposition there can be no ...

- righteousness or wickedness
- holiness or misery
- good or bad
- life or death
- corruption or incorruption
- happiness or misery
- sense or insensibility

The necessity of opposites leads right to the throne of God. Without contrast, none of God's great characteristics would exist because there would be no opposite to measure it against, no opposite to define it, no opposite that confirms its existence. As Lehi puts it, "If these things are not, there is no God. And if there is no God we are not, neither the earth; for there could have been no creation of things, neither to act nor to be acted upon: wherefore, all things must have vanished away."[49]

What a logic chain. Something exists and is affirmed when we can note its opposite. Something is defined not only by what it is, but by what it is not. One part of the opposing pairings helps to define the other part, and vice versa. Otherwise, "all things must needs be a compound in one" and nothing can exist. [50]

Contrasts and differences are subsets of the principle of opposition, and just as important. As opposites are necessary for our very existence, contrasts and differences are necessary for our progress. How well we learn the most profound difference in the universe – the difference between good and evil – determines our progress. Grasping this fundamental contrast and building on it is the pattern by which we can gain infinite knowledge.

We are taught "line upon line and precept upon precept, here a little and there a little"[51] – a gradual process with one piece of knowledge building on another. But this cannot happen without contrast. If the line or precept given today does not differ from the line or precept given yesterday, there is nothing to learn.

> Without contrast there is no education, no persuasion, no motivation, no growth – there is nothing.

Thus, in contrasts we have a principle that lies at the foundation of why we exist, and in contrasts and differences we have the foundation of all learning. That is why **our fellow occupants on this planet inherently want to know differences.** We should be only too glad to enlighten them.

So how does this apply to improving our image and spreading the gospel? As we choose our messages, two competing schools of thought are before us.

The commonality school says we should show the world the things we share in common – find common ground and explain how the circles overlap, so to speak. Because so many people have a distorted view of us, we should reassure them of the similarities in our characters and lifestyles. Then, as they become more accepting of and comfortable about us, the reasoning goes, they will be more open to investigating the gospel.

The contrast school says that people are motivated to investigate the Church when they discover a difference they find interesting, new, or unsettling. Contrast messages pointing out differences between religions have power because they imply something better, more logical, or more rewarding – e.g., our doctrines that God can still speak to His children for their benefit, or that the Godhead is not some amorphous cosmic muffin but is composed of three separate and distinct Personages. This school champions contrast because it causes discomfort in a positive sense. Comfortable people don't act. **It is the tension of contrasts that moves them.**

> The Church of Jesus Christ of Latter-day Saints has many beliefs in common with other Christian churches. But we have differences, and those differences explain why we send missionaries to other Christians[52]
>
> - Elder Dallin H. Oaks

There is, of course, nothing wrong with being liked, and we all wish the distortions about us did not exist. But commonality messages do not go far enough. A commonality by itself – for example, we're Christians, too – will not interest people in the Church. In his book *Here We Stand*, Joseph Fielding McConkie relates the story of how members in one branch tried the commonality approach with an investigator:

He was a very intelligent and fine man who was active in the Catholic faith. During the meeting the branch members did everything they could think of to convince this man that we, as Latter-day Saints, were just like him. They succeeded. At the end of the meeting he got up, walked out the door, and never came back. He told the missionaries on the way out he could see no reason to leave an established church to join one that was trying so hard to be just like what he already had.[53]

As long as we emphasize the commonality approach, we always will remain ineffective and wishy-washy. We can state our contrasting claims without apology and without arrogance, but state them we must. After Captain Moroni wrote his title of liberty[54] and invited all to join him, he did not run around the neighborhood seeking points of commonality with those who disagreed with his position. He didn't want soldiers who would wither in the heat of battle. He planted his banner – in contrast to the wisdom of his world – and there he stood.

> No candidate wins political office by saying that he's as good as the incumbent. He wins by drawing comparisons, by showing contrasts, by convincing people he offers something better.

So it must be with us. **We must politely disturb the status quo.** The Lord's people have always been a people apart, by definition different. So why should we try to be the same as others? We are different and to pretend otherwise is to be untrue to the re-established doctrines the Savior has revealed. Find the truths that other religions cannot or will not say, and put them into the conversation.

Differences pique interest. **People investigate things that are different, not things that are the same.**

Reframe the Issue

If someone repeats a false claim they've heard (you're not Christians, you practice polygamy, you don't believe the Bible), or poses a cynical question, don't become defensive. **View it as an opportunity** to place a new fact on a mental map.

When people say we're not Christians or that we worship a different Jesus, we often unwisely accept their framing and we argue the point:

"We are, too, Christians. Look at the name of our church. Read our first Article of Faith. Look at the writing on our buildings."

"You're not." "We are." "You're not." "We are."

That's Sandbox 101, and it's an unproductive debate. Imagine that this argument continues for several months and then your verbal sparring partner gives up and says, "Okay, you win. I'll accept you Mormons as Christians." And you say, "Great, now come investigate our church." And he'll say, "Why? You're a Christian and I'm a Christian. Why should I change?"

Little is gained from such an exchange. The best we can hope for in such a debate is to get back to square one.

But what happens if, instead of arguing whether we're Christians or not, we inject our simple claim into the discussion? Now our friends, if they are honest, will reason: "Wait a minute. Mormons claim to be the original Christian church. I don't know if they are or not, but if they claim to be the original Christians, it tells me at the very least that they have to be Christians. If Mormons are not Christians, why would they claim to be the original of something they are not?"

> If certain people do not accept us as Christians, so be it. Who made them the arbiters of Christianity? What matters is that people think about our claim. Whether others accept us into their tree-house club is immaterial. We know Whom we worship.

Mere exposure to our claim inoculates people against the commonly heard charge against us. In time, this reasoning process at the *individual* level will change the frame of the *public* debate about us, as well. Instead of "Are Mormons Christians?" the discussion will become "Are Mormons the original Christians?" Now that's a discussion worth having.

The same reframing principle applies when people question whether we believe the Bible. Our usual response is, "Yes, of course we do." And then we proceed to point out that we use the King James version, that we study it in Sunday school, and so on. But the framing remains the same: "Do Mormons believe the Bible, yes or no?" – and that means the best we can do is battle to a draw. My suggestion is that we refuse to play that game and instead change the framing by saying something like, "Yes, of course we do. In fact, we believe we are members of the same religion as those who wrote it."

This prods people to think outside traditional boxes. It puts a new thought in their minds which connects to our claim to be the original church – the organization based on the authority of all the holy prophets going back to Adam. And that's the kind of fact-planting that generates the deeper thinking that leads a person from curiosity to interest.

I hope these examples show that it does little good to accept the framing and playing field demarcated by a hostile questioner. We must **expand the person's vision of the issue** by introducing additional facts, drawing parallels, and emphasizing a different perspective. As an example, some people, intentionally uncouth or innocently ignorant, may question us about temple garments. To address these questions in the same framing as they are posed is to risk speaking lightly of sacred things. A good friend of mine, Paul Ashton, suggests answering such questions with a question: "Why do you wear a wedding ring? Isn't it to remind you of the promises you have made – promises of fidelity, love, and service?" Sometimes, referring to a parallel situation is all that is needed. Other times a follow-up statement may be in order: "We wear special garments to remind us of the promises of honesty, morality, and service we have made to the Lord."

Correct Distortions

Most of us Mormons love a religious discussion, but we are often less than adept at opening one. We have come to believe that starting such a discussion requires us to leave our comfort zones and boldly state some truth, and we're hesitant to do that. Fortunately, current events are making it easier for us by expanding our comfort zones.

The key is connectivity – how does our statement tie in with the ongoing conversation? Here we must think of two types of ongoing conversations – the *immediate* conversation, such as occurs with work colleagues around the water cooler, and the *public* conversation, such as what has been in the news recently. We will not feel uncomfortable if our comments can reasonably be connected to either of these two conversations. In fact, finding a connection to an issue or event already in the public arena has become substantially easier in the past few months.

While unconnected comments may get us stamped as crackpots, responding to something already in the public spotlight is understood by listeners to be relevant commentary. If we reference a news story or distortion about us in the media, we have established our connectivity, and **it is socially acceptable to set the record straight**. So if we find a distortion and respond to it, we are not leaving our comfort zones because people accept that we have the right to defend our religion, and may be surprised if we don't.

In other words, **negative comments from the world actually expand our comfort zones!**

> Elder Dallin H. Oaks spoke of those who misrepresent our beliefs ". . . and even revile us because of them. When we encounter such misrepresentations, we have a duty to speak out to clarify our doctrine and what we believe. We should be the ones to state our beliefs rather than allowing others the final word in misrepresenting them." [55]

Each of us must plan our own ways of commenting that fit our personalities, but here is a general pattern:

Ask a question that demonstrates connectivity to the public conversation about Mormonism: Did you see the article in the newspaper...? Have you heard about that new movie. . .? Did you hear what Reverend X said on TV last night. . .?

Then review the facts involved: The article said that Mormons. . . . The movie claims that. . . . Reverend X said. . .

Then offer an editorial comment: Sounds like the newspaper's fact-checkers were on vacation . . . Same worn-out cliches. . . . Whatever happened to civil discourse?

And let the matter go at that. **Let it float**. Perhaps a substantial conversation will follow. Or maybe our listeners will choose not to respond to our comments, but by the next time we talk, maybe a new item will have appeared in the public conversation and they may then have questions. Remember that one person in three would not mind learning more about us if the information came from a friend and if they were assured that they would not be pressured.

A productive conversation need not always have a resolution; in fact, the best way to generate interest is *not* to resolve every discussion.

Consider in this light the six distortion factors affecting our image. As our conversations move beyond delivering our basic claims to mental mailboxes, we may have opportunities to talk about specific distortions. Here are a few examples of primary and supporting comments that provide information, reassurance that we have no ulterior motives such as desire for power or domination, and that many things said and written about us are not true.

Factors that Affect Our Image and Examples of Conversational Comments	
Image Factor / Charges Against Us	**Conversation Comments / Response Ideas**
The Ignorance Factor	**Response Comments**

Mormons are not Christians. They are a cult.	We Mormons claim to be the re-established original Christian church.
	    Christ organized a church;
	    Men changed it;
	    Jesus Christ has brought it back.
	We believe Joseph Smith saw and talked with God the Father and His Son Jesus Christ.
	We are not historical Christians; we are New Testament Christians. We do not accept the creeds that men wrote 300 years after Christ's crucifixion.
	Why would we claim to be the original of something if we are not at least the something?

Mormons do not believe the Bible.	We believe the Bible because we claim to follow the same religion as those who wrote it
Mormons worship Joseph Smith.	Joseph Smith occupied the same position in today's church that Peter the Apostle occupied in the New Testament church. We no more worship Joseph Smith than the early Christians worshipped Peter.
Mormons worship a different Jesus.	We worship Jesus Christ as the Son of God, the promised Messiah, and our Savior who atoned for our sins, died on the cross, and was resurrected on the third day. There can be no different Jesus.
The Polygamy Factor	**Response Comments**
Mormons practice polygamy.	Polygamy has not been approved or practiced by the Church for more than 100 years. Any Mormon found to be practicing polygamy is excommunicated. Over 150 groups have broken away from The Church of Jesus Christ of Latter-day Saints, some of which practice polygamy. We do not recognize, protect, or affiliate with any of them. We do not hold Roman Catholics responsible for those who broke away from the Roman Catholic Church, and we are not responsible for those who broke away from ours.
Mormons tolerate and ignore polygamy practiced in their communities.	No church has the right to take upon itself governmental power. Polygamy is illegal, and it is the responsibility of civil authorities to enforce the law.

Factors that Affect Our Image and Examples of Conversational Comments

Image Factor / Charges Against Us	Conversation Comments / Response Ideas
The Power Factor	**Response Comments**
Mormons want power. If they get enough power, they will try to force people to convert.	God does not force anyone to do anything, and neither do we. A major doctrine of our church is individual agency – the freedom to choose. We will always defend the right of others to worship how, where, or what they may. Force has no place in our church, either in our members' lives or the lives of others. Everything about our Church is voluntary and based on the free will of the individual.
The LDS Church is rich and powerful.	Most of our church's wealth is in its meetinghouses. These are income-using rather than income-producing assets.
The Secretive Factor	**Response Comments**
Mormons have secret and mysterious ceremonies in their temple. What are they trying to hide?	God's people have always established sacred places where they can commune with God and learn more of Him. Anyone can enter our *temples* to worship God and Jesus Christ if he or she believes we are the re-established original Christian church, joins the Church, and keeps Christ's commandments. Anyone can enter our *meetinghouses* to worship God and Jesus Christ even if he or she does not believe we are the re-established Church. We are an open and welcoming religion. We encourage everybody to attend our Sunday meetings and ask us questions.
The Weird Factor	**Response Comments**
Mormons have weird and bizarre beliefs.	We Mormons believe we're normal people, but we are different in that we try to follow Christ's commandments instead of the practices of the world. Every religion appears weird to somebody. God's work has always appeared weird at first. Noah, Abraham, and Moses were definitely seen as weird at times to those around them. In the interest of fair play, the next time your minister tells you about our supposedly weird beliefs, ask him to invite one of us to tell our side of the story.
The Exclusionary Factor	**Response Comments**
Mormons believe they are the only ones who will go to heaven.	No one will be given any heavenly blessing or reward that is not offered to everyone else. People of all religious persuasions are children of God and He loves all of us.
Mormons believe God talks only to their prophet.	We believe God hears everyone's prayers. We believe God speaks to each of His children, no matter their religion, through their minds and hearts, to guide their individual lives. We believe He speaks to a prophet to guide the Church as a whole. If God spoke to Moses or Peter, why wouldn't He speak to a prophet today?

Of these distortions, the "Power Factor" requires our greatest effort. One of our greatest challenges in the years ahead as our membership grows and we become more visible will be to **assure our fellow citizens that they have nothing to fear** from us. Consider three statements we make, how they may be misconstrued, and how we might better explain what we mean.

Three Important Misconceptions to Correct		
What We Say	**What Some Hear**	**What We Mean**
We are the true Church.	Only Mormons are going to heaven. The rest of you are going to hell.	God is not a God of confusion. Churches with competing doctrines cannot each be correct. There can be only one true Church.
		All of God's children will have a fair opportunity, either here or in the life to come, to accept or reject Christ and His teachings.
We hold the authority to act in God's name.	Mormons believe they have the right to punish others and will do so if they have a chance.	We hold the authority to perform ordinances, such as baptism and eternal marriage, which will be valid and recognized in heaven. Individuals always have the right to choose whether to accept these ordinances.
		We do not have, we do not claim to have, nor do we seek any authority or power to force anyone to do anything.
The prophet of our church receives continuous revelation from God.	Only Mormons have a conduit to heaven. God answers only Mormon prayers.	There are two types of revelation.
		Personal revelation comes to an individual for use in his or her own life and can be received by anyone of whatever religion.
		Church revelation comes to a prophet, like Abraham or Moses, who then tells the Church and the world what God would have us do.

Four points need to be made here. **First**, though we make bold claims regarding the authenticity of our religion, **the doctrines of Christ preclude any use of force** to advance His church. While this goes without saying in our membership circles, we must take time to *clearly explain* this principle to others – that claiming we are the only true Church authorized to perform ordinances and teach in God's name does not give us any political, governmental, or societal power. Explaining this important truth is crucial to advancing the work.

Second, **we must emphasize our commitment to agency** and freedom of choice. Few people have heard of the eleventh of our thirteen Articles of Faith:

> We claim the privilege of worshiping Almighty God according to the dictates of our own conscience, and allow all men the same privilege, let them worship how, where, or what they may.

Third, we are no threat to taking over anything, even if we were so inclined. The Book of Mormon points out our situation in the last days – everywhere, but small – hardly a description of a threatening coalition of people:

And it came to pass that I beheld the church of the Lamb of God, and its numbers were few . . . [and] the church of the Lamb, who were the saints of God, were also upon all the face of the earth; and their dominions upon the face of the earth were small . . .[56]

If someone wanted to build a high-force movement, he would not begin by establishing an expectation that the movement's numbers will always be small.

Fourth, our bold message does not presage any use of political force. Our leaders state at almost every General Conference that this Church is the only true and living church on the face of the earth, as President Henry B. Eyring unequivocally did in the April 2008 conference. We carry that bold claim to the world and we cannot dilute it. But our firm position can in no way be equated with force. Knowing the principles upon which our church is based, I can state unequivocally that if the president were a Mormon, all 100 senators and 435 representatives were Mormons, and the whole Supreme Court were made up of Mormons, Americans would not see any use of political power to force people to convert.

We believe Jesus Christ is the head of this Church, and He never will force anyone to join it or to keep His commandments.

If we correct distortions and provide clear information, many honorable people will come to our defense when we are attacked, though they themselves may never join the Church.

An enthusiastic returned missionary, Matt Moyer, was taking his lunch break at work when a co-worker commented that a lot of Mormons had been put in jail somewhere in Texas. "I slammed down my ham sandwich," he said, "and told him, 'We need to talk.'" Thus began a lengthy discussion about who is a Mormon and what doctrines we

accept and do not accept. Moyer thou   vas the end of it, but a week later, the co-worker said to him,   ded your church, Matt. My minister preached against you Mor   Sunday. After the service, I went up to him and said, 'Rev   ou're wrong about the Mormons' and told him everything you

We need more such friends. And they will step forward, defend us against unfair attacks, and help improve our image **to the extent they understand why we believe as we do**.

135

Use Technology

> I do not feel obliged to believe that the same God who has endowed us with sense, reason, and intellect has intended us to forgo their use.

- Galileo

Terry Jeffers, a friend since BYU days, has spent many hours in Christian chat rooms. He says that when he first started, he had a tendency to preach and found that others fired bullets in return. Once he decided to just answer questions about the Church, he found a lot of friends. He maintains that people are on religious websites for both social and informational reasons, which is why it's called social networking. They're interested in information, but only when he relaxes and chats with them do his efforts to help the Church become fruitful.

Work from Comfort Zones

When a possibility arises to converse about religion with those of other faiths, many of us freeze up because we think this requires a foray outside our warm and fuzzy comfort zone, and we don't want to leave it. We're not unusual in that regard, of course; no one loves discomfort, and it is the exceptional person who willingly leaves his comfort zone for any extended time. So how is it done?

- We do it by *expanding* our comfort zone, as mentioned earlier, not by *leaving* it.
- We do it when we use the Internet, email, text messaging, and whatever will be invented next.
- We do it when we recognize that improving our image is easier than doing regular missionary work.

When a sensitive topic such as religion is discussed, a successful interaction with those of other faiths requires three conditions:

A safe opening — People want a comfortable beginning – a natural conversation -- that is not awkward. A simple fact, delivered touch-and-go or parenthetically, will not be clumsy or embarrassing. As stated previously, negative statements about us legitimize discussion of our religion and make it easier for us. They provide a safe opening for further discussion. If certain people and media outlets weren't attacking us, we'd want to invent them.

A safe harbor — Few of us are secure enough to leave our comfort zones. We prefer being on our own turf, away from the storms of daily life. Our home is our safe harbor.

A safe interface — When our friends are cocooned in their safe harbors and we are in ours, email conversations are comfortable. We do not have to look at each other face to face and be brilliant conversationalists immediately and spontaneously. We can weigh our words and compose messages at our leisure that can be sent from one safe harbor to another.

An email conversation gets around the fears one or both parties experience when religion is mentioned – fear of pressure, loss of friendship, inadequate knowledge, embarrassment, undermined beliefs, diminished self-image, among others – because cyber communication respects comfort zones and provides us with sufficient time to compose thoughtful questions and answers.

The key to never leaving our comfort zones is an email conversation.

> For $5 ($125 in today's money), the Pony Express in 1860 would deliver a one-ounce letter 2000 miles. It would take ten days if the weather cooperated.

Consider today's technological opportunities from the viewpoint of someone who is curious to learn more, but fears pressure and wants to do it at a distance. We could, of course, suggest that he go to mormon.org and take a chance he'll find what he wants, ... or we could become the facilitator and provide information tailored to his needs. While mormon.org is a useful resource, and we hope that those who do not know an active member of the Church will browse it for information, merely driving people to the site is like dropping off a busload of tourists at Temple Square without a guide. People don't need someone to point them to a website; **they need a friend with whom to trade emails.**

The written word carries power. If you have ever sorted through the effects of a deceased relative, you were probably surprised how many letters were kept over the years and undoubtedly read and re-read. There is something about a written letter or simple note from a friend or loved one that is so special.

Letters have for centuries been the prime method of conveying things of importance, from deeply held feelings to brilliant scientific insights. Consider just a few people in history who carried on deep and interesting correspondences:

Heloise and Abelard

John and Abigail Adams

Adams and Jefferson

Goethe and Carlyle

Emerson and Thoreau

Browning and Barrett

Tchaikovsky and von Meck

Even had they had the opportunity to meet daily or weekly face-to-face, these famous letter-writers would probably still have corresponded with the written word. They would still have committed their thoughts to paper because there's something about composing just the right words that **facilitates a soul-to-soul communication**.

With Tchaikovsky, it was all pen and ink – more than 1200 letters. Over the thirteen years of their correspondence, he never met his confidante and benefactress, Nadezhda von Meck. Adams and Jefferson, another example, wrote hundreds of letters commenting on deep ethical, moral, and political issues, and did so even when they were political enemies.

> The war in heaven was fought with words.
> They are conveyors of information and the building blocks of logic chains and argumentation.

Written words live because they can be read, re-read, and pondered, which is all the more reason to use email conversations to communicate serious information about the gospel. The simple, written word has always been the vehicle to deeper understanding, and remains so today if we will but use it. Writings from the heart can now be transmitted at the touch of a button – we have the best of both worlds.

Let's say you're at the office, school, or neighborhood barbecue and you comment to a friend or colleague about a news article, the political scene, a sermon, or a movie – things that reference the Church. How do you turn a moment of easy conversation or light repartee into an email conversation?

First of all, do not feel you must provide information then and there. Bring up one or two things that fit naturally into the conversation and if they pick up on it, then volunteer that you have background information – a review, an article, a statistic – that you could email them.

"I'll send you some background information on that."

"I don't have a ready answer on that point, but I'll find it and email it to you, if you'd like."

"I don't know where these rumors come from. For whatever reasons, some people tell stories about us that are not true. Let me email you an explanation I read a few days ago."

"Let me send you a review I read of that movie."

"Let me send you our side of the story."

"We Mormons haven't done a very good job of telling people who we are and what we believe, so let me send you a short article I think will correct distortions about that."

"A friend sent me a list of the ten most frequently asked questions about Mormons. I'll forward it to you."

If specific questions arise, offer to send a *short* explanation. This may also be the time to promise that if they have other questions, you'll answer them, no more and no less.

> Email means never having to say you're uncomfortable.

Remember that **people are more comfortable discussing religious topics by email than face to face**, so they should welcome information by email. It also takes the pressure off both parties to think on their feet.

Create an E-Library

So now you have a friend who gives you his email address and says, "Okay, send me something." What's the next step?

As you become comfortable with this new approach to spreading the gospel, you should build your own E-Library – a file of interesting facts, statements, quotes, articles, and other explanations about the Church. Here are the guidelines:

- Except when you add a newspaper article or similar document to your library, keep each file short, perhaps only one to four paragraphs of text. Lists, such as an FAQ or a compilation of famous Mormons, can, of course, be longer.

- Resist the temptation to quote long excerpts from the *Encyclopedia of Mormonism*. The more ideas you can couch in your own words, the greater the soul-to-soul communication.

- De-jargonize it. It is acceptable to draw from Church manuals, but make sure any unique words we use are defined or replaced with words that those of other faiths will recognize.

- As you prepare your files, build short, medium, and longer-length attachments for various levels of religious interest and understanding.

- Do not post your E-Library on a website and direct your friends to it. Write your emails as you would talk to your friend, and then carefully select appropriate information to attach. People are more likely to open an email attachment than click on a link.

As you prepare an email, you have a choice of embedding information in your text or tacking it to your missive as an attachment. If it's short, incorporate it; if longer, include it as an attachment.

It would be easy for me to send you my own E-Library, but I would be cheating you out of two blessings. First, if you create a personalized library, you will use it. And second, if you build your own collection of useful items, **you will gain a confidence that will extend both downstream and upstream** – that is, you will be confident in ongoing email conversations and you will become more confident when you first meet someone. Knowing that you have a library of solid information supporting you will make you more adept at dropping comments into conversations and asking your listeners if they would like to receive additional information by email.

Remember that when presenting facts by email, there is ...

> ... no fear of embarrassment
> ... no fear of ridicule
> ... no fear of losing a friend
> ... no fear of being viewed unfavorably

... and there is no fear of saying the wrong thing because you will be backed up by your own collection of well-developed facts and explanations.

But here's what I will do. To begin your own E-Library, send your email address to me at office@lds-elibrary.com and I will send you a starter kit (pass the e-munition) of three items that I have found quite popular and especially easy to offer to pass along to others:

> Mormon FAQ
> Well-known Mormons
> Weird things Mormons believe

Through email discussions, we first become tour guides as we facilitate a personal, comfortable, ongoing Q&A with our friends, and in time, mentors as their curiosity turns to interest.

Write Something

We as members may not be able to afford ads in the local newspapers, but we can submit letters to the editor and respond to comments on the Internet for free. Whether we write to local newspapers or on a blog, the idea is to respond to articles about us with stimulating facts and rhetorical questions. Here are two examples.

Responding to a comment about whether or not we're Christians:

In a recent (article) (posting), the question came up, "Are Mormons Christians?" The answer depends on your definition.

Mormons follow New Testament Christianity and believe theirs is the re-established original Christian church. They believe Jesus Christ is the Son of God and offers the only path to salvation. They believe Christ organized a church when He was on the earth. It adhered to His doctrines and His ordinances, such as baptism. It was His perfect organization, built upon prophets and apostles.

Mormons believe that men changed the original church following Christ's crucifixion and the deaths of the apostles. They reject the changes that Greek philosophy and Roman power injected into Christianity.

So, if Christian means subscribing to *historical* Christianity, including the creeds men developed 300 years after Christ's ministry, then Mormons would not be historical Christians. But if Christian means subscribing to the *original* church that Christ organized, then the argument is over. The organization, ordinances, and doctrines of The Church of Jesus Christ of Latter-day Saints more closely mirror New Testament Christianity than do those of any other church.

Responding to a comment on whether Mormons believe in the Bible:

In (an article that appeared in your paper last _____) (a posting by _____), the question came up whether Mormons believe in the Bible. The answer is: Of course we do; we belong to the same religion as those who wrote it.

Here's the logic. Mormons claim that Christ organized a church, that men changed it, and that it has now been re-established. So if we claim to be the re-established original Church of Jesus Christ, why *wouldn't* we believe in the scriptures that came from that original church?

The original church in New Testament times and the re-established church today are two manifestations of the same organization, separated only by 1700 years when all of the true Christian doctrines were not on the earth. Members in New Testament times and members today were and are members of the same church ... with the same doctrines, organization, ordinances, and authority to act in Christ's name.

That's why the official name of the church today is The Church of Jesus Christ of *Latter-day* Saints (saints meaning members) to distinguish between the two time periods of Christ's church.

So not only *do* Mormons believe in the Bible, they necessarily must believe in the Bible. After all, we're members of the same church as the authors.

Answering questions in fresh and unexpected ways will enlarge the boundaries of the debate, cause buzz, and force the opposition to defend its own claims.

Sow the Threads

A thread is a sequence of postings on an Internet forum by contributors who comment on a news article, blog, event, or discussion. We sow threads by posting our claim and a few facts.

At BYU-Hawaii's graduation ceremony in December 2007, Elder M. Russell Ballard called on members of the Church to use new technology, and whatever is yet to be invented through the inspiration of the Lord, to join a worldwide conversation about the gospel:

> There are conversations going on about the Church constantly. Those conversations will continue whether or not we choose to participate in them. ... I ask that you join the conversation by participating on the Internet, particularly the "new media," to share the gospel and to explain in simple, clear terms the message of the Restoration. ... Perhaps now, more than ever, we have a major responsibility as Latter-day Saints to define ourselves, instead of letting others define us.[57]

There are numerous ways to contribute to the conversation:

- **Visit websites** of news outlets and watch for reports about the Church or its members. Newspaper websites as a category attract the most readers, although Yahoo News.com has twice the unique visitors per month as the largest single newspaper site, the New York Times.[58]

- **Search for blogs** that have open-thread conversations about the Church and comment as appropriate.

- **Start your own blog**. Tell the story of how you became converted and what the re-established Church – the full restored gospel – means to you. Invite readers to submit questions for you to answer.

- **Download videos** from Church websites and add them to your E-Library to be shared with friends as appropriate.

Here are a few suggestions, principles, and Internet etiquette guidelines:

- Manners of regular conversation apply. Be courteous and polite. Keep your comments relevant to the material under discussion.

- Once you identify yourself as a member of the Church, or even if you don't but your comment defends it, you de facto represent the Church. Others will judge all of us by what you write. It should go without saying that all of our contributions to the worldwide conversation must be respectful of others' opinions, deficient in factual foundation though some may be.

- Keep it civil and use such phrases as "I respect your opinion, but I must disagree with it" and "We can disagree without being disagreeable."

> Why not call ourselves on Internet thread-sowing missions?

- Keep in mind that somewhere in each conversational thread is a person who would like to know the truth.

- Don't be afraid to correct an inaccuracy, but be sure you have the facts. A charge against the Church left answered will in time be accepted as true.

- When someone attacks us, take advantage of your expanded comfort zone to respond. We have a right to correct distortions; in fact, it's expected.

- Remember, people have a right to their own opinions about us, but they do not have a right to their own facts. Clear facts make strong postings.

- A point is driven home if more than one Church member in a thread refutes the same distortion, each in his or her own words.

- The easiest form of persuasion is the correction of a distortion. If you come upon an antagonistic thread about the Church or find an offensive comment that indicates ignorance of the facts, correct the distortion clearly and with kindness. Your calm voice will be appreciated by those looking for the truth, even though other posters may pummel you.

- Short postings are read most.

- Our message is already bold. All we need do is post it so it will find its way to the right mental mailboxes.

- Compliment news organizations and other blogs when they post fair and accurate articles about us. Paying a compliment is a form of planting facts.

- If you have a blog, provide an easy way for people to comment and/or contact you.

- It is permissible to mention your own blog in a comment on someone else's blog, but it is considered better form if a friend references you in his comment. In either case, the reference should be followed by a link to your site.

- It is permissible to place your email address in a comment on a thread if you are willing to entertain contacts for more information. An invitation to correspond is most effective when you have posted a strong comment, but it's apparent that more should be said. One way to put it might be: "I don't want to hog the thread with a long explanation, so if anyone would like a deeper discussion, please contact me at. . . ."

- If a thread appears to be attracting considerate and respectful comments, and if you don't have your own blog, offer your email address and welcome questions. It's best to use a separate email account rather than the one you use with family and friends in case you get swamped.

- To cut down on spam, some bloggers spell out the symbols in their email addresses as, for example, gary [at] parameterfoundation [dot] com.

We have strong messages to share, but our credibility as messengers slides if our writing contains misspellings and grammatical errors. Spellcheck each posting and check carefully for agreement betw[een] nouns and verbs before hitting the Send button. As for other de[tails,] here are the most misused words in threads and the correct def[initions] to guide you:

Your	Possessive, as in "your book"
You're	Contraction meaning "you are"
Its	Possessive, as in "He didn't know its power."
It's	Contraction meaning "it is"
To	Preposition, as in "go to work"
Too	Meaning also, as in "I like it, too."
	Also indicates excess, as in "too biased"
There	Designation of a location, as in "over there"
Their	Possessive, as in "their beliefs"
They're	Contraction meaning "they are"
Loose	Adjective, as in "a loose knot"
Lose	Verb, as in "He will lose the argument."
Who's	Contraction meaning "who is"
Whose	Possessive, as in "Whose book is this?"

Thousands of members, each working one conversation at a time across the Internet spectrum, **can change perceptions as effectively as an expensive mass-media campaign**, perhaps even more effectively.

> Consider the power of each one of us, [13] million strong, of our own free will and choice reaching out to those not yet of our faith in unconditional friendship. [59]
>
> - Elder Marlin K. Jensen

Guide Patiently

Time was invented so everything wouldn't happen at once.

Our best opportunity to improve our image comes when people get to know a solid, active member of the Church. Because there are 49 Americans of other faiths (or no faith at all) for every Mormon, we need to significantly increase the opportunities for more Americans to get to know us. There are only two ways for this to happen: current members must do more and/or we must convert more members – a multiplier effect, as it were.

This seventh and last step discusses what happens when the curious become interested and the interested become ready to seriously investigate the Church, as 5% of Americans can already visualize themselves doing. It focuses on how we facilitate investigation of the Church in such a way that when people are ready to join, they will be models of our ideals, true Christians in every sense of the word ... and by the lives they lead, improve the image of The Church of Jesus Christ of Latter-day Saints.

The key is gentle mentoring. To mentor means to coach, assist, inform, advise, watch over, facilitate, help, guide, counsel, suggest, and teach. Mentoring carries a tone of kindness, patience, wisdom, long-suffering, love, empathy, experience, and selflessness. It is natural, not forced.

The Mentor Approach

Political geography sounded like an interesting class and I had a group to fill, so I thought, why not? It turned out to be the most exciting learning experience of my academic career and a wonderful example of what a mentor can accomplish.

Dr. Russell Horiuchi of BYU was a mentor teacher, not a data-dump teacher. He presented the basic information we needed, of course, but it was the questions he posed in class that exercised our mental muscles, prodded us to connect the dots, and prepared us for ... The Final.

The Final consisted of a map, a few sheets of statistics, and several questions we had to answer.

The map showed a dozen fictitious countries, topography, longitudes and latitudes, rivers, ore deposits, harbors, forests, plains, etc.

The sheaf of statistics listed populations, age distributions, education levels, economic indicators, and the production tonnages of about 20 commodities for each of the countries.

The test itself asked: Which countries will trade with each other? Which countries will form which kinds of political systems and why? Which countries will form alliances and why? Who will fight whom, and who will win? Justify your reasoning.

It was an open-book test, we could work with whomever we wished, and we had 72 hours to complete it. Larry Eastland, Richard Sharp, and I must have worked 60 of those 72 hours. We were on fire; time meant nothing, and food was only fuel. "What will this country do with its manganese deposits?" "Who needs wool?" "Do harbors freeze at the 50th parallel?" "If this country has bauxite, where will it get its energy to smelt aluminum?" And on and on and on. When the test was over we were drained, exhausted, and exhilarated. We owned that fictitious world. We knew it backwards and forwards.

We had become our own teachers. Rather than being told how the dots were connected, we had to find those connections ourselves. To this day, I still remember discovering that manganese is used to harden steel (something no self-respecting social scientist should be expected to know), and that the country with manganese is likely to team up with the country with iron ore deposits so they can both make tanks. If Dr. Horiuchi had just told me that fact, I would've remembered it about three seconds. But because I had to work, because I discovered it on my own, and because I had to think about the implications, that factoid has stuck with me.

This experience taught me the powerful techniques of a mentor teacher:

- Provide enough information to _trigger curiosity_, but not so much that all the student must do is listen;

- Fan interest with _stimulating questions_ so that the student wants to find the answers;

- Let the student _connect the dots_ and analyze the meaning;

- Realize that knowledge sticks when the student must _work_ for it. This in turn teaches the student how to teach himself and how to study on his own;

- Encourage the student to _take ownership_; it's his journey, not the teacher's.

Professor Horiuchi was a mentor first class because he helped us discover facts and connections, and we took ownership. I believe the above principles are great guidelines to follow in our efforts to spread the gospel.

Another powerful mentor teacher I was privileged to observe was my
bishop while I was in graduate school. From my own experience and
from talking with others in the ward, I learned that his *modus operandi*
was consistent. He would ask how we were doing and then listen
intently to whatever problem was on our minds, asking questions so he
would understand where our heads and hearts were. What surprised
many ward members was what he would say after he understood the
problems for which we came to him for assistance. He would not tell
us what to do because he knew that if we searched our own knowledge
and testimonies, the solution was usually within our range to discover.
Rather, he would ask, "What is *your* game plan and how can I help?"
Notice that his prime question – what is your game plan? – is the essence
of the mentor approach. He did not take ownership of our problems by
telling us the solutions, although in most cases he no doubt knew what
we had to do. No, we owned the monkey going in, and we owned
it coming out. He signaled he would play only a *supporting* role.
We exercised our agency, we took ownership, and we grew.

His example of how to help people grow and solve problems was a
pattern I used when I was a bishop counseling members, though, alas,
not with his brilliance and deep empathy. (One member of my ward only
half-jokingly told me that my philosophy seemed to be "Solve your own
problem, but do keep in touch.") No former member of the Stanford
Ward was surprised in the least when years later that mentoring bishop
was called as an apostle and that he now sits in the First Presidency.
Thank you, President Henry B. Eyring.

Mentor Without Pressure

To appreciate how carefully we must guard against pressure entering into our religious conversations, recall the six-stage model discussed in Step Two – awareness, awakening, curiosity, interest, investigation, and conversion. There are three critical distinctions in this stair-step process.

First, **awakening is not curiosity**. It is simply a recognition that something is going on, that the Church has attracted attention for whatever reasons. If we assume awakening is curiosity, we may provide more information than a person is ready to assimilate.

Second, **curiosity is not interest**. We sometimes assume that a person asking a question is interested in the Church, whereas he or she may only be interested in a small amount of information. As Elder M. Russell Ballard told us in the October 2007 General Conference:

> The most common request we hear is a fairly simple one that goes something like this: "Tell me a little about your Church." The key word here is "little." They are not saying, "Tell me everything you know and then send others to tell me everything else ..." [W]e need to remember that there is a difference between interest and mere curiosity. [60]

Those who assume curiosity is interest may prematurely suggest a formal teaching situation, and the person may interpret this as pressure and back away.

Third, **interest is not investigation**. An interested person will listen, but an investigator will study. Interest must be nurtured from a passive to an active state. If we assume interest is investigation, we may attempt to harvest the fruit before it is ripe, and the person may either be scared off or agree to baptism and later become inactive.

Interest may lead to baptism, but gently nurtured investigation is more likely to result in true conversion. Those baptized while only in the interest stage may not have thoroughly considered and met the conditions of D&C 20:37 – humility, desire, broken heart, contrite spirit, true repentance, willingness to take upon them the name of Christ, determination to serve Him, and works which manifest that they have received of His spirit.

Converts are more likely to remain steadfast in their conversion after solid investigation and sincere soul searching, steps we must not rush or overlook. The active investigator is better equipped to become an active member. **True investigation takes work and the assistance of a gentle mentor.**

Fellow LDS pollster Ron Hinckley tells the story of his son, Dan, who befriended John, the non-member husband of a sister in his ward, and continued the friendship by email and phone calls long after the family moved to another state. As John's oldest child approached baptism age, a more serious consideration of the Church led him to his conversion. He called Dan and asked if he would fly out to baptize and confirm him, to which Dan responded, "Why me?" John answered, "Because in all the time we've known each other, you were the only person who did not try to convert me, who was just my friend and showed me the gospel by example."

Some Church members feel that they must be assertive in their religious conversations with others. They feel that bold behavior and pushing are appropriate ways to kindle interest. I do not. I am a strong believer in non-pressure methods of spreading the gospel. If we assertively enter into conversations determined to get referrals, we may get lucky, but I doubt this is a common way that lasting converts start their conversion journey. In my experience, the best referrals – those that lead to conversion, not just baptism – are those which flow naturally from unhurried friendships and proceed through non-pressured investigations.

When an interviewer asked a woman from Tennessee what three questions she would ask about Mormonism, the woman said something more fitting to this book than she could possibly have known. After stating that she would like to know whether Mormons believe in Jesus Christ as their Savior, she said, "I would love to find out anything about their church, but it should naturally evolve from the conversation."

Our message is sufficiently assertive by itself if we simply state it in clear language. Rather than being bold messengers with a gentle message, we are much further ahead being **gentle messengers with a bold message** because the Explorer personality, open-minded and tolerant of dissonance, appreciates a non-pressured presentation of facts to weigh and analyze.

> If the Savior had been concerned that people might be offended by His message, He never would have appeared to Joseph in the grove.

Of course, our message will offend some people; this has been true throughout history. Some will be offended because of the way we state our message, and others will be offended no matter how it's presented, even if the Savior Himself were to deliver it. We can't do much about the latter, but we can help the former by explaining our position without arrogance, self-righteousness, or condescension. And if this approach is not successful, the decision to be offended is theirs, not ours, especially if we are not acting in a pushy, offensive way.

The effectiveness of our presentation lies in the boldness of our message, not the pressure of the presenter.

A mentor skillfully suggests.

Rather than asking, "Will you read this chapter?", a mentor will say, "Here's another chapter you might find interesting."

Rather than asking, "Will you come to Church?", a mentor will say, "Any time you'd like to visit our worship services, you're surely welcome."

Rather than saying, "Will you quit smoking?", a mentor will ask, "What can I do to help you give up cigarettes?"

By the same token, a well-mentored friend is more likely to act, not promise to act. If membership is to be, he will make all the necessary commitments on his timetable, not ours.

Help Friends Take Ownership

A young Russian woman, Marina Popova, attended Southern Utah University and naturally enough was soon being pushed to join the Church. She was interested, but in no hurry to commit to a baptismal date. She told me, "When I investigated on my own, that's when I made progress. I didn't want to get baptized for the wrong reasons. I didn't want pressure; I wanted to do it by myself." Marina joined the Church on her time schedule, married in the temple, and is very active in her ward.

Similarly, a convert in my stake, Sandy Heathcote, says that it took work for her to really understand the Book of Mormon, as well as feel what she was reading. "I needed it to make sense in my mind and sense in my heart because once it becomes understood and familiar, then you really start building a testimony. Those words need to become a part of you, but it doesn't happen unless you study them. Otherwise you can't get that depth that allows you to stay." The Book of Mormon isn't called our best missionary for nothing.

Own the investigation, own the testimony.

> . . . acquiring a testimony is not a passive thing but a process in which we are expected to *do* something.[61] [Emphasis in the original.]
>
> - Elder Dallin H. Oaks

This principle should not come as a surprise. **We value things we must work for**. If little or no effort is expended, we don't appreciate what we've been given. We buy into and bond with those things we must work and sacrifice to achieve.

If an investigator's knowledge of the gospel is a series of facts he absorbed as he passively listened to the missionaries, if he has not studied on his own, and if he has not thought about the implications of those facts, his chances of remaining an active member are slim. He will not have taken ownership. *He will always feel that he's in someone else's church.*

If, however, a member asks that investigator to think about the implications of the presented facts, has helped the person connect the dots and discover the connections that give fire to knowledge, and has guided that person to become his own teacher, then that convert will be a solid member for life. He will have taken ownership. *The Church will become <u>his</u> church because he will have his own testimony.*

> If investigators do not work to gain a testimony, why should we expect them to put their shoulders to the wheel after they're baptized?

As we answer questions and provide information, we may be tempted to take control of the conversation. We must do exactly the opposite and **put control and ownership in the hands of our friends.** Let them guide the conversation and work to *their needs*, not ours. If they are in control, though it will require more patience on our part, they are more likely to continue their investigation.

I had been on my mission to South Germany 18 months when I met Leopold and Anni Demel, a couple in their 30s. Though cordial, Anni was not interested in our message, but Leopold was and said we were welcome to come as often as we wanted as long as we followed his ground rules: One person speaks at a time; you will tell me your position and I will tell you mine; you will answer my questions; you will not push me; we will have a civil discussion, not an argument. Fair enough, I thought; at least we had a live one. "By the way," he said, "the Jehovah's

Witnesses lasted for one meeting and the Seventh-Day Adventists came twice." And so we began.

The missionary program at the time was an introductory lesson followed by six memorized lessons in a rapid-fire Q&A dialogue. My companion and I dutifully followed the script for about half of the first lesson before Anni stopped the canned discussion and said indignantly, "Did you come here to play school master or to tell us about your religion?" We mumbled some explanation, but Anni marched out of the room anyway, never to be involved in our discussions again (although she hospitably fed us every time we visited).

My companion and I decided a change might possibly be in order. We then and there ceased being lock-step executors of the script and became mentors instead.

Leopold Demel was 15 when World War II broke out and three years later was inducted into the Luftwaffe. Intelligent and Germanic-logical, he would have been an engineer or doctor under more favorable circumstances, but his chances for an education came to a halt when the war began and were put further out of reach when he was captured by Soviet forces near the end of the conflict and spent three years as a POW.

Leopold was the epitome of a curious explorer. He would ask us to state one of our beliefs, would ask questions to make sure he understood our position, then would present his viewpoint, ask us for evidence for ours, counter with other views he had heard, then pause and say, "*Moment mal* (just a moment)." We came to understand that this was his signal that he now needed time to send out mental feelers to connect and properly place the new information we had provided on his mental map, and in the right mailbox.

Sometimes the thinking time would be a few seconds, other times a half hour or more. Absolute silence. He would then say one of two things: "*Akzeptiert* (accepted)" or "*Noch nicht* (not yet)." With ruthless analytical precision, he marched through every gospel concept we could think of, sorting the information like bricks into two piles – *Akzeptiert* and *Noch nicht* – until one evening some three months later when he had traveled as far as his mental abilities would take him and was hung up. All of the bricks were in the *Akzeptiert* pile except two – tithing and prayer – and he couldn't budge them. I told him not to worry about tithing but to concentrate on prayer. I said he had a beautiful intellectual testimony of the gospel, but it had no fire. "Concentrate on communicating with your Heavenly Father," I told him, "and when you receive an answer for the big pile of bricks, a testimony of tithing and prayer will come with it."

Two months later his prayers were finally answered, but instead of applying for baptism, he said, "I know how far I can go without my wife. You must allow me time to explain the gospel to her in my way." We were in complete agreement. For the next seven months, Leopold treated Anni like the curious explorer he was himself. When she would ask, "What do your Mormons think about such-and-such?", he would answer her question and volunteer nothing further. *She guided the conversations in sync with her needs.* Gradually, Anni Demel warmed to the message of the restoration, was the one who suggested they exit the Catholic Church (a formal procedure because of state-withheld church taxes), and was the one to suggest a baptism date. The whole process from the time we knocked on their door until their baptism was one year.

In the intervening years, the Demels have faithfully filled numerous callings, Leopold as branch president on several occasions and as a member of the Stuttgart Stake high council, Anni as Relief Society president and as stake Primary president. Two more-converted people cannot be found. But their investigation of the Church and their lives in a small branch in an antagonistic city have not been easy. When we met them, the priests and ministers in their half-Catholic-half-Lutheran city were unified in preaching against us, sending mailers and harassing families we were teaching.

But the Demels not only survived, they thrived. What I learned from this seminal experience of my mission is that ...

- We must be flexible and sensitive to how *the investigator* wants to proceed;

- Lasting converts are those who *take ownership* of the investigation process and study;

- We must be in tune with what the Spirit prompts *us* to do and not compare our efforts with the way someone else may be advancing the gospel; and

- God's children are as *different and unique* as snowflakes – no two are alike, and therefore no two approaches should be alike.

Allow Time

Participants in my national survey were asked whether, if they were facing a major decision in their lives, they would go with their first feelings and intuition or would prefer to think about it for a while. By an 81% to 17% margin, people said they would prefer to think about it rather than make a first-intuition decision.

I do not doubt that there are strong members of the Church who converted as adults in a short period of time. But whenever I have asked obviously solid converts how long they investigated before joining, most answer the question in months or years, not weeks or days. To bring more of these dedicated people into the Church takes time because **mentoring takes time**.

> Brigham Young took two years to investigate the Church. Parley Pratt, on the other hand, required less than two days to become converted. But during that time, Parley studied intensely, even foregoing sleep. Intense study is the only substitute for time.

Consider the following three time factors within the conversion journey and the time the average person needs to convert, especially those who are deliberate in their decisions.

Time to learn. The beauty of the gospel is that its basic doctrines can be understood at any level of mental capacity, but it is also true that the more a person knows about the gospel, the less he will be swayed by family or friends trotting out falsehoods and challenges to our beliefs. We are counseled to read the scriptures daily so we will have both the mental and spiritual strength to resist the cunning of the adversary. From the time the sons of Mosiah became converted until they left on their missions, they invested considerable effort learning the doctrine, as we are told they "waxed strong in the knowledge of the truth; for they were men of a sound understanding and they had searched the scriptures diligently. . ."[62]

The same principle must surely apply to investigators in our day. The more time they take to learn the gospel, the stronger their testimony and the less likely they are to suffer buyer's remorse after they join.

Time to connect the dots. The gospel is a collection of interconnected truths. Knowing individual facts is only the first step. Those investigating the Church must come to understand how these truths are connected and discover for themselves what these connections imply for their own lives. For example, an investigator might ponder, "If the Book of Mormon is true, that must mean that Joseph Smith was indeed a prophet, which means that he did see the Father and the Son, which means that this Church is the repository of the pure teachings and principles of Jesus Christ, which means I must live according to these principles if I wish to please Him."

We can explain such logic chains to investigators in a matter of minutes, but it takes time for them to internalize these truths and figure out the implications for their own lives, and only they can do it. (Of course, the Spirit can accelerate this process, but in most cases only after the investigator has exerted himself and studied diligently.) Even after coming to a knowledge of the truth, many investigators will require additional time to build the necessary courage to act upon it.

Time to ponder. We gather facts by *reading* and listening. We connect the dots on our mental maps by *studying*. We give this knowledge fire by pondering and *experimenting* on the word.

The word *ponder* appears in twelve verses of scripture, and in eight of them the pondering takes place in the heart. This suggests something much deeper than casual listening or a few fleeting thoughts; it is the deep thinking as a concept is "taken to heart." This deep effort is critical to the building of a testimony because **work is required to become anchored** in the gospel. The Holy Ghost may verify that a teaching is true, but it does not automatically follow that a testimony has been built.

Alma's advice to the Zoramite poor was consistent with the way Explorers, our potential lasting converts, process information – with faith, diligence, and patience. It took time for these Zoramites to awake and arouse their faculties, experiment upon Alma's words, exercise a particle of faith, have a desire to believe, and let that desire work in them.[63] Seeds in the heart take time to stir, grow, bloom, and take root.

As our friends move from curiosity to interest and then to investigation, we will not only be asking them to change their religion, but their culture, habits, social activities – indeed, their entire way of life. They will need **time to understand, connect, internalize, and act**. Gentle mentoring allows investigators time to do all of these things and thus build testimonies of their own.

> In business or family matters, those making major decisions take time to analyze situations from all angles before committing to one path or another. Can we expect anything less of people regarding the life-changing covenants we are asking them to make?

Onward and Upward

 Therefore, behold, I will proceed to do a marvelous work among this people, even a marvelous work and a wonder. . . .

- Isaiah 29:14

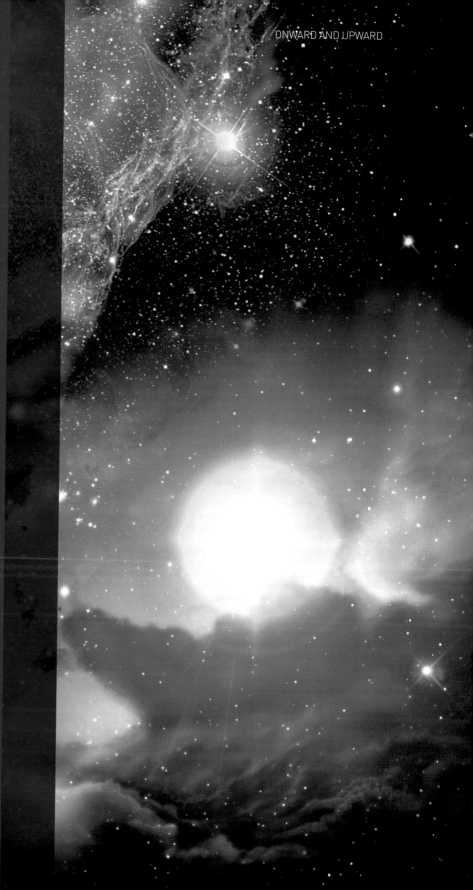

For behold, this is my work and my glory—to bring to pass the immortality and eternal life of man.

- Moses 1:39

If I were asked to identify the most important takeaways from this book, they would be these:

- We have a poor public image and it will not improve by itself. It needs the help of each member.

- We will improve our image as we place facts in mental mailboxes in the course of friendly and natural conversations.

- Mass media messages can take us only so far. The final steps in educating the American public about who we are and what we believe falls upon us members through our lives and our comments.

- Before we comment, we must listen.

- Speak plainly and follow the Golden Rule.

- The nucleus message we must deliver, in words that anyone can understand, is that we claim to be the re-established original Christian church.

- A bold message delivered gently is more effective than a gentle message delivered boldly.

- Disturb the status quo kindly. Our message is already bold.

- Pointing out similarities of beliefs may make us feel good, but pointing out differences stirs interest.

- There is no learning without contrast.

- A sizeable segment of Americans fears that we have a power agenda to force our beliefs on others.

- Telling people that force has no place in the church and that we are committed to freedom of choice and the principle of individual agency is critical to allaying fears and improving our image.

- Pressure tactics in the investigation process are counterproductive.

- Over 65,000,000 Americans – more than ten times our current membership – would be interested in learning more about Mormonism from a member if they were assured they would not be pressured.

- Mistaken identities and false beliefs about polygamy are a major impediment to interest in the Church, and we must not be shy about correcting those distortions.

- Because of negative buzz, we can spread the gospel without leaving our comfort zones.

- Let the curious and the interested take control of the learning process.

- Gentle mentoring produces long-lasting converts who will then add their efforts to ours to improve our image.

The Savior has said that for the elect's sake He will hasten His work in its time and shorten the days before His Second Coming. The corollary is that Satan will also hasten his work, for he knows his days are numbered. Events will trigger major changes in the fortunes of our efforts to spread the gospel.

Saturday, August 12, 1961, was just another boring day of getting doors slammed in our faces. We were tracting in a particularly antagonistic neighborhood in a south German city, and I can't remember that we were invited into a single home or had any substantive talk with anyone at the door.

The next morning, the East German communist government began building the Berlin Wall. My companion and I were busy with ward business on that Sunday, so we didn't get back on the doors until Monday morning when all of Germany was holding its breath. Picking up where we left off two nights before, we began our daily routine. It was the best day of tracting I had on my whole mission. Where someone was home, we got into every single door. Every single door from 9:00 in the morning until about 2:30 in the afternoon: "Come on in. The name's Schmidt – S-c-h-m-i-d-t. Just in case you guys are right and we all get vaporized within the next few hours, please remember me up in heaven."

Of course, nobody got poofed, and even if Herr Schmidt had joined that very day, he would not have lasted. Before long, the Schmidts and Muellers of the world returned to their curious habit of demonstrating to Mormon elders how much force a door jamb could take without breaking.

I have mused on this incident many times since. Quick conversions arising from fear do not last, but fearful events can stimulate interest, which can be nurtured through gentle mentorship. Someday the Lord will preach His own sermons, and they will have substantially greater impact on the world than the building of the Berlin Wall. When He does, the environment will change and things will be seen in a different light. The blinders the world has placed over the eyes of many will be lifted, and they will recognize things as they truly are.

We can help prepare the world for that day. We can help reach the 25% who already have indicated that they are curious, interested, or could see themselves seriously investigating the Church. We can be like Alma the Elder who, though he did not know it for years, was successful in planting one key concept in his son's mind which Alma the Younger recalls in Alma 36:

> . . . I remembered also to have heard my father prophesy to the people concerning the coming of one Jesus Christ. . . . Now, as my mind caught hold upon this thought . . . . I could remember my pains no more. . . .[64]

That thought had been planted many years before, but did not take hold until Alma's environment changed, the appearance of an angel accompanied by earthquakes definitely qualifying as an environment-changing event. When it did take hold, Alma knew what he had to do. His father's words, lying dormant in one of Alma's mental mailboxes for a very long time, eventually saved him.

So it can be with our messages. We must continue to state our claim and drop facts into natural conversations. **Some people will act on them now and some will act on them when the environment changes**.

But one thing is sure. Between now and the Second Coming of the Savior, **environments _will_ change and tides _will_ turn**, and people will draw upon what they know and what they have heard to try to make sense of both the marvels and the upheavals. What may be camouflaged today will in time be seen in bold relief. The Church will come out of the wilderness – become more visible and bless the lives of others – perhaps directly proportional to the number of people who know an active member of the Church who has placed an orienting thought in their mental mailboxes.

> "I remember a Mormon I met at a community meeting. Seemed like a good guy. He said they claim to be the re-established original Christian church. Maybe I'd better check them out."

Notes and Bibliography

1. Lawrence Research, Santa Ana, CA, February 16-23, 2008. N=1000 adults proportionate to population density in the 50 states using random digit dialing to give all residents, whether their telephones had listed or unlisted numbers, an equal chance of being chosen to be interviewed. Margin of error is ±3.1 percentage points for mid-range reported results.

2. Gallup Poll. 22-25 Feb. 2007. www.gallup.com/poll.

3. See, for example, www.liveprayer.com/ddarchive3.cfm?id=2931.

4. Ballard, M. Russell. "Faith, Family, Facts, and Fruits." Ensign. Nov. 2007: 25-27.

5. Prothero, Stephen. Religious Literacy; What Every American Needs to Know – and Doesn't. San Francisco: Harper, 2007. 1.

6. Prothero, 30. The original sources are detailed on page 252.

7. The Pew Forum on Religion and Public Life. 1-18 Aug. 2007. N=1461 for questions about Mormonism. Full results may be found at www.pewforum.org. The words in each category were:

   Negative Responses (27%) Wrong / False / Not Christian / Polygamy / Cult / Crazy / Strange / Weird / Deceptive / Manipulative / Exclusionary Secretive / Aggressive / Pushy / Bigoted / Racist / Sexist / Extreme / Radical / Rigid / Restrictive

   Positive Responses (23%) Devout / Faithful / Religious / Family / Family Values / Caring / Kind / Sincere / Good People / Religious / Community / Unity / Close-Knit / True / Truth

   Neutral Responses (19%) Different / Unusual / Strict / Abstinence / Utah / Salt Lake City / Neutral / Fine / OK / Christian / Jesus / God / Proselytizing / Missionaries / Confusing / Mysterious / Complex / Joseph Smith / Brigham Young / Organized / Structured / Conservative / Money / Wealth

8. Eyring, Henry. Reflections of a Scientist. Salt Lake: Deseret Book, 1983. 46.

9. Gallup Poll. 22-25 Feb. 2007. www.gallup.com/poll.

10. "View of God Can Predict Values, Politics." USA Today 12 Sept. 2006. Quoting a Baylor University mail-out poll conducted in the fall of 2005.

11. 2 Nephi 25:23.

12. Novak, Robert D. "A Mormon in the Oval Office?" Washington Post 4 Oct. 2007. Web.

13. Winder, Michael K. Presidents and Prophets, American Fork: Covenant Communications, 2007. 125.

14. Barbarak, Mark Z. "Iowa's Last Word on Politics." Los Angeles Times 7 Sept. 2007.

15. "Are Americans Ready for a Mormon President?" Los Angeles Times 2 July 2006.

16. Alter, Jonathan. "The Race Is On." Newsweek 25 Dec. 2006.

17. Gallup Poll. 9-11 Feb. 2007. www.gallup.com/poll.

18. Gallup Poll. 6-9 Dec. 2007. www.gallup.com/poll.

19. Poll. 20-22 Jan. 2008. Wall Street Journal / NBC. http://online.wsj.com.

20. Ballard, M. Russell. "Faith, Family, Facts, and Fruits." Ensign. Nov. 2007: 25-27.

21. U.S. Religious Landscape Survey. The Pew Forum on Religion and Public Life. May-Aug. 2007. Released Feb 2008. www.pewforum.org.

22. Hinckley, Gordon B. Stand a Little Taller. Salt Lake: Eagle Gate, 2001. 214.

23. Ballard, M. Russell. "O Be Wise." Ensign. Nov. 2006: 17-20.

24. Ephesians 2:20; 3:11.

25. McBrien, Richard P. Encyclopedia of Catholicism. New York: Harper Collins, 1995. 1147.

26. McBrien. 1155.

27. 1 Corinthians 14: 4, 19.

28. Ballard, Nov. 2007.

29. Prothero, Stephen. Religious Literacy; What Every American Needs to Know – and Doesn't. San Francisco: Harper, 2007. 1.

30. Oaks, Dallin H. "Sharing the Gospel." Ensign. Nov. 2007: 7.

31. Hinckley, Gordon B. Stand a Little Taller. 322.

32. JSH 1:33. I've always considered this, Joseph's first prophecy, as another indication of his prophetic mantle. What other teenager would say he would be known for both good and evil? Many youth visualize themselves being known someday for some great and positive achievement, but to state in a matter of fact manner that he would be known also for evil flies against human nature at that age. It had to be something he was told.

33. Ballard, Nov. 2007.

34. Ballard, Nov. 2007.

35. Acts 17:21-23.

36. Alma 17-18.

37. Richards, Franklin D. "Prepare to be Leaders." BYU Devotional. 16 Mar. 1976. Address.

38. Holland, Jeffrey R. "The Only True God and Jesus Christ Whom He Hath Sent." Ensign. Nov. 2007: 40-42.

39. Holland, Jeffrey R. "My Words ... Never Cease." Ensign. May 2008: 91-94.

40. D&C 123:12.

41. 2 Nephi 29:3.

42. Montague, Terry Bohle. "Mine Angels Round About." Orem, Utah: Granite Publishing, 1989. 97-100.

43. Stack, Peggy Fletcher. "Mitt's bid for White House took the pulse of nation on Mormonism." Salt Lake Tribune 8 Feb. 2008.

44. D&C 38:41.

45. Alma 37:6.

46. Hinckley, Gordon B. Interview. Church News 1 Sept, 1995.

47. Quoted in a Deseret News story upon his death, January 27, 2008.

48. 2 Nephi 2.

49. 2 Nephi 2:13.

50. 2 Nephi 2:11.

51. 2 Nephi 28:30.

52. Oaks, Dallin H. "Apostasy and Restoration." Ensign. May, 1995: 84.

53. McConkie, Joseph Fielding. Here We Stand. Salt Lake: Deseret Book, 1995. 5.

54. Alma 46.

55. Oaks, Dallin H. "Testimony." Ensign. May 2008. 26-29.

56. 1 Nephi 14:12.

57. Ballard, M. Russell. "Using New Media to Support the Work of the Church." Graduation, Laie, Hawaii. 15 Dec. 2007. Address. May be accessed at www.lds.org.

58. Nielson Online. The top five newspaper websites are: NYTimes.com; USATODAY.com; washingtonpost.com; Newsday.com; and WSJ.com (Wall Street Journal).

59. Jensen, Marlin K. "Friendship: A Gospel Principle." Ensign. May 1999: 64.

60. Ballard, Nov. 2007.

61. Oaks, May 2008.

62. Alma 17:2.

63. Alma 32:27.

64. Alma 36:17-19.